Diabetic Air Fryer Cookbook

Diabetic Air Fryer Cookbook: 1500-Day Easy and Mouthwatering Recipes for Living Healthier and with More Energy. Boost Your Well-Being without Sacrificing Taste. Includes 30-Day Meal Plan

Melissa Jordon

ANTI-INFLAMMATORY COOKBOOK FOR BEGINNERS

1200 Days of Simple Recipes to Heal the Immune System, Live Healthy and Reduce your Body Inflammation

MELISSA JORDON

THIS BOOK INCLUDES A
FREE BONUS

The "Anti-Inflammatory cookbook for beginners" is **100% FREE**, and all you need to get it is a name and an email address. **It's super simple !**

TO DOWNLOAD THE BONUS SCAN
THE QR CODE BELOW OR GO TO

https://melissajordon.me/bonus-da/

SCAN ME

MELISSA JORDON
— collection —

Table of Contents

Introduction

What Is an Air Fryer?

An air fryer can bake and roast like an oven, but the difference is that it has heating elements on top, which results in a more efficient cooking process with fewer oil splatters and a higher temperature than a conventional oven. While an oven bakes and roasts food, an air fryer does so by heating it with a smaller compartment filled with heat-generating elements and a powerful fan located on top.

You can fry just about anything in air fryers. From frozen chicken wings and homemade French fries to roasted vegetables and fresh-baked cookies, there is something for everyone. This device has become popular in recent years, with nearly 40% of U.S. homes having one because it is easy to use, and cleanup is a breeze. Usually, you can wash your cooker in the dishwasher.

How does it work?

Air fryers come in different sizes, shapes, and prices. It has two key components: a drawer where food goes and a basket or grate that elevates and holds the food. The heating element heats up oil or fat as it circulates around, causing it to heat up too quickly.

The air fryer uses hot air, which surrounds the food and cooks it thoroughly. The top panel of an air fryer has a heating mechanism and fan; the fan keeps air moving over the element so that hot air can escape cleanly; if not, smoke could form inside your appliance. When turned on, hot air rushes down around the food in a basket-style fryer. When air is heated, it expands and cools. That process, known as convection, causes hot air to rise and cause the surface of a food product to cook.

Then comes the basket, an essential part of the design: it allows hot air to circulate around the food without being blocked like the pan or cookie sheet used in a traditional oven.

Is Air Fryer Good for Diabetics?

Air frying is healthier than traditional frying because it reduces the fat and calories typically added when frying in oil. So, in that sense, air-fried foods are a better choice for diabetics than traditional fried foods.

An air fryer cooks food using less fat than conventional methods; therefore, it shouldn't have a special effect on diabetics. Fat doesn't raise blood sugar levels as carbohydrates do, so anyone with type-2 diabetes should be able to eat air-fried foods as long as the food itself doesn't contain excess carbohydrates and still maintain stable blood sugar levels.

Note that an air fryer doesn't magically transform unhealthy foods into nutrient-rich wonders for our bodies; you can still make smart choices when using it. Always read labels and talk to your dietitian to find out what's in the food you're cooking.

CHAPTER 1: Breakfast

1. Hard-Boiled Eggs

Preparation time: 10 minutes

Cooking time: 15 minutes

Servings: 4

Ingredients:

• 4 eggs

Directions:

1. Allow the air fryer to preheat at 275°F. Take the tray and place the eggs on it. Make sure you place them in a single layer and cook for 15 minutes.

2. Remove them from the fryer, rinse with cold water, place in ice water until completely cooled, drain and refrigerate until ready to use. If desired, cut each egg before serving.

Per serving: Calories: 72 Kcal; Fat: 5 g; Carbs: 0 g; Protein: 6 g; Sugar: 0 g; Sodium: 71 mg

2. Crisp Egg Cups

Preparation time: 5 minutes

Cooking time: 13 minutes

Servings: 2

Ingredients:

• 1/8 teaspoon salt
• Cooking spray
• 2 slices whole wheat bread
• 1/8 teaspoon black pepper
• ½ tablespoon trans-fat free tub margarine
• 1/2 slice deli style ham
• 2 large eggs

Directions:

1. Set the air fryer temperature to 375°F and leave to preheat. Spray 4 custard cups or ramekins with nonstick cooking spray.

2. Crusts from the bread are not needed for now, just remove them and save them for other use.

3. Spread a layer of margarine on one side of each piece of bread (it should be a thin layer).

4. Place bread in cups, pressing gently to shape bread to cup. Repeat three times.

5. Slice ham into strips about 1⁄2-inch wide. Place strips in single layer into cups.

6. Crack an egg into each cup, along with salt and pepper to taste.

7. Place filled cups in the basket and cook until eggs are softly set or as desired (10–13 minutes).

8. Carefully remove ramekins from the basket, holding ramekins carefully by their sides so you don't accidentally break them when removing them from the basket; run a knife around the sides to transfer onto the plate while still holding ramekins by the sides; use a hot pad to hold ceramic plate steady while sliding it out of the basket; set on countertop safely away from heat source.

Per serving: Calories: 150 Kcal; Fat: 8 g; Carbs: 6 g; Protein: 12 g; Sugar: 1 g; Sodium: 410 mg

3. Hash Browns

Preparation time: 5 minutes

Cooking time: 8 minutes

Servings: 4

Ingredients:

• 4 Potatoes (Medium sized)
• ¼ Tablespoon freshly ground black pepper
• 1 Tablespoon oil
• ½ teaspoon salt

Directions:

1. To make hash browns, shred the potatoes in a food processor. Put them into a colander and place them under cold water for 1 minute. Drain the colander for a few minutes.

2. Transfer the shredded potatoes to a clean paper towel and press them dry. Make sure to dry them out completely for the crispiest hash browns.

3. Add oil and seasonings to the bowl; mix well before adding to the basket of air fryer set at 380°F for 15 minutes. Flip the basket over and repeat on the other side until desired crispness is reached (it should take another 5-10 minutes).

4. **Per serving:** Calories: 195 Kcal; Fat: 4g; Carbs: 37g; Protein: 4g; Sugar: 2g; Sodium: 304mg

4. Egg in a Hole

Preparation time: 5 minutes

Cooking time: 8 minutes

Servings: 1

Ingredients:

- 2 Eggs
- Salt
- Pepper
- 1 Tablespoon butter
- Bread (2 Slices)

Directions:

1. First, preheat your air fryer to 325° F for 3 minutes.

2. Place a parchment paper round in the basket and butter on both sides of the bread.

3. Use a glass, or you can use a cookie cutter to cut a hole in the center of the bread.

4. Crack an egg into the hole, season with salt and pepper, then cook at 325° F for 6 minutes.

5. Remove from the air fryer and serve.

5. Breakfast Potatoes

Preparation time: 5 minutes

Cooking time: 20 minutes

Servings: 6

Ingredients:

- 3 Bite-sized cut Potatoes
- ½ Diced bell pepper
- 1 Teaspoon garlic powder
- 1 Teaspoon Onion Powder
- Salt and Pepper (To taste)
- 1 Tablespoon Extra Virgin Olive oil
- Parsley

Directions:

1. To make Air-Fried Breakfast Potatoes, preheat the air fryer to 380°F.

2. Then wash and scrub the potatoes and cut them into bite-sized pieces with the skin on.

3. Pat them dry with paper towels, then transfer them to a large bowl.

4. Add spices; coat with olive oil, and stir to combine well.

5. Add bell pepper; stir to combine well (garnish with parsley for added color!).

6. Cook for 20 minutes or until the desired level of crispness. Shake and turn potatoes halfway through cook time to ensure even browning (shaking may cause chips to sizzle).

7. **Per serving:** Calories: 111Kcal; Fat: 2g; Carbs: 21g; Protein: 3g; Sugar: 1g; Sodium: 782mg

6. Sausage biscuit

Preparation time: 5 minutes

Cooking time: 20 minutes

Servings: 2

Ingredients:

- 2 Eggs
- ½ Pound sausage
- ½ Teaspoon salt
- ¼ Teaspoon Pepper
- ½ Tablespoon butter
- 1 Can Grand Biscuits
- ¼ Cup Cheddar Cheese

Directions:

1. Place a skillet/pan over medium-high heat and brown the sausage, breaking it into crumbles.

2. Then whisk the eggs with salt and pepper and cook them in butter over medium heat until they are soft and scrambled.

3. The eggs will continue to cook inside the biscuits as you cook them.

4. Preheat the air fryer to 350°F for 5 minutes.

5. Remove one biscuit from the can and pull apart the layers. Top half of it with cheese, eggs, and sausage.

6. Next, top with remaining biscuits and pinch seams together to seal each packet.

7. Place them in the air fryer with space between them, so they don't touch one another.

8. Cook them for 5 minutes at 350°F or until golden brown.

9. **Per serving:** Calories: 153Kcal; Fat: 12g; Carbs: 4g; Protein: 8g; Sugar: 1g; Sodium: 480mg

7. Prosciutto and Spinach Egg Cups

Preparation time: 7 minutes

Cooking time: 10 minutes

Servings: 6

Ingredients:

• ½ Cup baby Spinach

• 6 Slices of Prosciutto

• ¼ Teaspoons of salt and pepper

• 6 Eggs

Directions:

1. Set the temperature of the air fryer to 375°F (190°C). Spray or drizzle the muffin tin with oil, then lay one piece of prosciutto inside each cup.

2. Gently press about 4-5 spinach leaves into the bottom of each cup.

3. Crack and add eggs into cups, one egg for each cup, and sprinkle with a little pepper; they're ready to go into the air fryer.

4. Carefully transfer your muffin tin or muffin cups to the air fryer (do not fill up completely), close, and cook for 10 minutes.

5. **Per serving:** Calories: 97Kcal; Fat: 7g; Carbs: 1g; Protein: 7g; Sugar: 1g; Sodium: 214mg

8. Air Fried Bacon

Preparation time: 5 minutes

Cooking time: 10 minutes

Servings: 5

Ingredients:

• 1 pound Bacon Slices

Directions:

1. Heat up the air fryer to 400 °F for 5 minutes.

2. Place 5 pieces of bacon in the air fryer or as many as your air fryer can hold. It's ok if they overlap slightly since they'll shrink down.

3. Set the cooking time for 10 minutes. After 5 minutes of cook time, check the bacon and adjust as necessary if you prefer more crispy bacon or thinner slices of bacon, cook for another 1-2 minutes. Thicker-cut bacon might take longer than thinner ones to cook through.

Per serving: Calories: 531Kcal; Fat: 1.9g; Carbs: 38g; Protein: 112mg; Sugar: 0.0g; Sodium: 1910mg

9. Bagels

Preparation time: 10 minutes

Cooking time: 15 minutes

Servings: 4

Ingredients:

• 1 Cup Greek yogurt

• 1 Egg

• 1 Cup Flour (Self-Rising)

• ¼ cup sesame seeds

Directions:

1. Add the self-rising flour and Greek yogurt to a medium bowl; mix with a wooden spoon until combined.

2. Knead the dough on a generously floured surface for 5 minutes.

3. Divide the dough into 4 pieces and form each piece into a small rope; secure the ends together to form bagels.

4. Preheat the air fryer to 280 °F.

5. Once heated, spray the air fryer tray with non-stick spray; place bagels on the tray.

6. Brush with egg wash; sprinkle with sesame seeds if desired.

7. Bake them until the tops are golden brown; this would take roughly 15 mins.

8. Serve warm as is or toast if preferred.

Per serving: Calories: 148Kcal; Fat: 1g; Carbs: 25g; Protein: 10g; Sugar: 2g; Sodium: 22mg

10. Homemade Granola

Preparation time: 5 minutes

Cooking time: 15 minutes

Servings: 12

Ingredients:

- ½ Cup dried berries
- 3 Cups Rolled oats
- ¼ Cup pumpkin seeds
- ¼ Cup Honey
- ¼ Cup Chia seeds
- ½ Cup Almonds
- ¼ Cup olive oil
- ¼ Teaspoon Salt
- Pumpkin Spice

Directions:

1. This recipe combines oats, nuts, seeds, and pumpkin spice.

2. Pour the oil and honey into a bowl with the oat mixture, mixing well until everything is well coated.

3. Set the temperature of the air fryer to 350°F (160° C) and preheat it for 5 minutes.

4. Line a container with parchment paper and spread out the oat mixture in one layer use a spoon to press down evenly to ensure that it is even throughout.

5. Once done, keep it out until completely cooled, then break into clusters.

6. Add dried fruit if desired along with any additional add-ins, and mix well before storing in an airtight container after allowing it to cool completely.

Per serving: Calories: 215Kcal; Fat: 11g; Carbs: 26g; Protein: 5g; Sugar: 8g; Sodium: 42mg

11. Breakfast Frittata

Preparation time: 5 minutes

Cooking time: 16 minutes

Servings: 4

Ingredients:

- 4 Tablespoon Cheddar Cheese
- 4 Eggs
- 4 Mushrooms
- 1 Green Onion
- 3 Grape Tomatoes
- 3 Tablespoon Heavy cream
- 4 Tablespoon Spinach (Chopped)
- Salt
- 2 Tablespoons Fresh herbs

Directions:

1. To make a frittata, preheat the air fryer to 350°F / 180°C.

2. Line a deep baking pan with parchment paper, then oil the pan and set it aside.

3. Add the eggs and cream and whisk them together in a mixing bowl.

4. Add the remaining ingredients to the bowl, and stir them until combined.

5. Once the mixture is ready, pour it into the pan, then place it inside the air fryer basket.

6. Cook for 12-16 minutes, or until eggs are set; insert a toothpick in the center of the frittata and check for cleanness before serving.

Per serving: Calories: 147Kcal; Fat: 11g; Carbs: 3g; Protein: 9g; Sugar: 1g; Sodium: 133mg

12. Perfect Cinnamon Toast

Preparation time: 5 minutes

Cooking time: 5 minutes

Servings: 6

Ingredients:

- 2 Pinches of Black Pepper
- 1 Pinch salt
- 1 Stick Butter
- ½ Teaspoons Ground Cinnamon
- 12 Slices Bread
- ½ Cup sugar
- Vanilla

Directions:

1. To make an easy cinnamon roll, soften butter in a small saucepan over medium-low heat.

2. Add sugar, vanilla, and salt while the butter melts.

3. Stir until completely combined.

4. Spread one-sixth of the mixture onto the bread, making sure to cover the entire surface from end to end.

5. Place as many slices into your air fryer basket.

6. Cook at 400°F for 5 minutes.

7. Remove from Air Fryer and cut diagonally for a delicious treat!

Per serving: Calories: 335Kcal; Fat: 17g; Carbs: 45g; Protein: 6g; Sugar: 20g; Sodium: 432mg

13. Soft-Boiled Scotch Eggs

Preparation time: 28 minutes

Cooking time: 12 minutes

Servings: 6

Ingredients:

- 1 Pound pork sausage
- 6 Eggs
- 1 Cup Panko crumbs
- ½ Teaspoon garlic powder
- ½ Teaspoon chili powder
- 1 Tablespoon brown sugar
- ¼ Cup wondra

Directions:

1. To make a Scotch egg, you'll need a medium saucepan, some eggs, and cold water.

2. Fill the saucepan halfway with water and bring to a boil over medium-high heat.

3. Remove cold eggs from the refrigerator and crack them into a bowl of ice water.

4. Use slotted spoons to carefully place them in boiling water; don't crowd the eggs in the pan.

5. Reduce heat and cover the pan.

6. Simmer for EXACTLY 6 minutes—no more than that, or your egg will cook too fast and become tough and tough.

7. While eggs are cooking, prepare an ice bath for the eggs in a large bowl; make sure it's big enough so your eggs won't touch each other when they're brought into it later on.

8. After 6 minutes, use the slotted spoon to remove cooked eggs from boiling water and immediately submerge them in the prepared ice bath for 10 minutes. The purpose of this step is to halt the cooking process, which is vital to achieving creamy, runny centers.

9. Gently roll each piece of sausage into a ball.

10. Place the balls in refrigerator for about 30 minutes.

11. Peel soft-boiled eggs and pat them dry with a paper towel.

12. Start with a cold sausage ball straight from the refrigerator.

13. Place meatball in center of 8x8 parchment square, gently pat down until you have an oval shape.

14. Gently lay egg on top of sausage oval; perpendicular to long sides of oval, gently pull away from parchment as you wrap around the egg with thick sausage points removed at ends.

15. For Breading Eggs

16. To make breaded eggs, you'll need three small bowls: one for your Wondra and garlic powder (Stir to combine), the second for beaten egg, and the third for Panko crumbs, brown sugar, and chili powder.

17. First, mix together flour with salt in bowl number one.

18. Then, shake off any excess.

19. Next, dip each sausage-covered egg in flour mixture and then into the beaten egg before rolling it in Panko crumbs.

20. Preheat your air fryer for 10 minutes at 380 °F.

21. Set the scotch eggs in the bottom of your air fryer basket, and make sure you leave enough space between each one so that air can circulate around it.

22. Air-fry eggs for 12 minutes, turning halfway through for more even browning.

Per serving: Calories: 342Kcal; Fat: 9g; Carbs: 7g; Protein: 19g; Sugar: 2g; Sodium: 591mg

14. Scrambled Eggs

Preparation time: 3 minutes

Cooking time: 9 minutes

Servings: 2

Ingredients:

- 1/8 Cup cheddar cheese
- 2 tablespoon milk
- 1/3 Tablespoon butter
- Salt and Pepper
- 2 Eggs

Directions:

1. Place butter in an oven-safe pan and place the pan inside the air fryer.

2. Cook at 300 °F until the butter has melted, about 2 minutes.

3. Take a small bowl and whisk eggs and milk, then add salt and pepper to taste.

4. Pour eggs into the pan and cook for 3 minutes; use a spatula to stir eggs inside the pan.

5. Cook the eggs for another 2-3 minutes, then add cheddar cheese, stirring again.

6. Cook for another 2 minutes before removing it from the air fryer. Serve immediately!

Per serving: Calories: 126Kcal; Fat: 9g; Carbs: 1g; Protein: 9g; Sugar: 0g; Sodium: 275mg

15. Cheesy Baked Eggs

Preparation time: 4 minutes

Cooking time: 16 minutes

Servings: 2

Ingredients:

- 4 Eggs
- Salt and pepper
- Smoked Gouda (Chopped)
- Everything bagel seasoning

Directions:

1. Spray ramekins with cooking spray.

2. In each ramekin, add one cracked egg and add 1 ounce of shredded Gouda to each ramekin.

3. Season it with some salt and pepper according to your taste.

4. Add your favorite everything bagel seasoning on top of each ramekin (as much as you like).

5. Place all four ramekins into the air fryer basket, then cook at 400 °F for 16 minutes until the eggs are cooked through.

Per serving: Calories: 240Kcal; Fat: 16g; Carbs: 1g; Protein: 12g; Sugar: 0g; Sodium: 270mg

16. Crispy Air Fryer French toast

Preparation time: 5 minutes

Cooking time: 6 minutes

Servings: 4

Ingredients:

- 12 Slices French bread
- 2 Eggs
- 1 Teaspoon Vanilla Extract
- 4 Tablespoons Maple syrup

- 2/3 Cup dairy milk
- ¾ Teaspoon cinnamon
- 1 Cup fresh blueberries, strawberries and raspberries.

Directions:

1. Set the temperature of your air fryer to 350 °F.

2. Lightly grease the air fryer with cooking spray or oil.

3. Place your eggs, milk, and vanilla in a large bowl and whisk until blended.

4. Dip the bread into the batter, letting any excess drip off before placing it on the rack of your air fryer.

5. Air fry for 3 minutes on each side until golden brown.

6. Serve it with some delicious maple syrup and fresh berries for breakfast!

Per serving: Calories: 229Kcal; Fat: 14g; Carbs: 18g; Protein: 8g; Sugar: 1g; Sodium: 203mg

17. Easy Air Fryer Omelet

Preparation time: 5 minutes

Cooking time: 10 minutes

Servings: 2

Ingredients:

- 2 Eggs
- ¼ Cup shredded cheese
- 1 Teaspoon Breakfast seasoning
- ¼ Cup milk
- Fresh Vegetables (Onions, Mushrooms, Bell pepper)
- Salt

Directions:

1. Take a small mixing bowl, add eggs and milk and mix them well until combined.

2. Add salt to the egg mixture according to your taste.

3. Add veggies to egg mixture.

4. Pour egg mixture into a well-greased 6"x3" pan.

5. Place pan in a basket of air fryer at 350°F for 8-10 minutes.

6. Halfway through cooking, sprinkle on breakfast seasoning and cheese.

7. Use a thin spatula to loosen omelet from sides of pan; transfer to plate and serve.

Per serving: Calories: 208Kcal; Fat: 12g; Carbs: 6g; Protein: 19g; Sugar: 3g; Sodium: 26mg

18. Breakfast Pizza

Preparation time: 5 minutes

Cooking time: 15 minutes

Servings: 4

Ingredients:

- Sausage (Crumbled)
- Crescent dough
- ½ Cup cheddar cheese
- ½ Cup mozzarella cheese
- 3 eggs (Scrambled)
- ½ Chopped pepper

Directions:

1. To make an air-fried breakfast pizza, spray a pie pan with oil, spread dough evenly in the pan, and place it in the air fryer.

2. Cook at 350°F for 5 minutes or until the top is slightly browned.

3. Remove from the air fryer.

4. Top with eggs, sausage, peppers, and cheese; then return to the air fryer for an additional 5-10 minutes or until golden brown.

Per serving: Calories: 250Kcal; Fat: 19g; Carbs: 5g; Protein: 14g; Sugar: 2g; Sodium: 424mg

19. Sweet Potato Hash

Preparation time: 15 minutes

Cooking time: 20 minutes

Servings: 4

Ingredients:

- 2 Tablespoon Brown sugar
- 2 Sweet potatoes

- 4 Strips of Bacon
- ½ Cup yellow onion (Diced)
- 2 Tablespoon Olive oil
- Salt and Pepper
- 1 Tablespoon Fresh rosemary

Directions:

1. To cook the sweet potato hash, preheat your air fryer to 400 °F.

2. In a small bowl, combine diced bacon with brown sugar and stir to coat; set aside.

3. In a larger mixing bowl, combine diced sweet potatoes with olive oil, rosemary, salt, and pepper.

4. Stir until potatoes are well coated.

5. Add mixture to preheated air fryer basket and cook for 8 minutes.

6. Open basket and stir again; add brown sugar-coated bacon; return to air fryer basket and cook until potatoes are lightly crispy on the outside and soft inside; this would take about 6 to 7 mins.

7. Serve and enjoy your amazing Sweet potato Hash.

Per serving: Calories: 199Kcal; Fat: 11g; Carbs: 20g; Protein: 5g; Sugar: 10g; Sodium: 349mg

20. Breakfast Egg Rolls

Preparation time: 10 minutes

Cooking time: 10 minutes

Servings: 4

Ingredients:

- 4 Eggs
- 1 Teaspoon butter
- 4 Slices cooked bacon
- ½ Cup cheddar cheese
- Salt and Pepper
- 4 Egg roll wrappers

Directions:

8. Prepare the air fryer and set the temperature to 390°F.

9. Crack the eggs into a small bowl, season with salt and pepper, and whisk until well blended.

10. Add the butter to a medium frying pan over medium heat.

11. Sprinkle cheddar cheese and crumbled bacon onto the top of the eggs and stir to combine until the eggs are cooked through.

12. Lay 1/4 of the egg mixture onto one end of each wrapper.

13. Roll up each egg roll away from you and seal each point with more water, if needed.

14. Repeat with the remaining 3 wrappers.

15. To ensure the egg rolls are cooked through and are not sticking to each other, put the egg rolls in the basket and make sure that they are not touching.

16. Lightly brush each egg roll with olive oil before air frying for 8 minutes.

Per serving: Calories: 258Kcal; Fat: 19g; Carbs: 8g; Protein: 13g; Sugar: 1g; Sodium: 370mg

CHAPTER 2: Sides and Vegetables

21. Potato Chips

Preparation time: 20 minutes

Cooking time: 15 minutes

Servings: 2

Ingredients:

- Minced fresh parsley
- 1/4 teaspoon sea salt
- 1 large potato
- Olive oil-flavored cooking spray

Directions:

1. Preheat the air fryer to 360°F. Use a vegetable peeler and cut potatoes into very thin slices. Transfer to a large bowl; add enough ice water to cover them. Soak for 15 minutes; drain them, add more ice water, and soak another 15 minutes.

2. Drain potatoes; place on towels to pat dry. Spritz them with cooking spray; sprinkle with salt. In batches, place potato slices in a single layer on greased trays in the air fryer basket.

3. Cook until crisp and golden brown, stirring and turning every 5-7 minutes if necessary. Sprinkle it with parsley if you feel like it.

Per serving: Calories: 148 Kcal; Fat: 1 g; Carbs: 32 g; Protein: 4 g; Sugar: 2 g; Sodium: 252 mg

22. Roasted Green Beans

Preparation time: 15 minutes

Cooking time: 20 minutes

Servings: 4

Ingredients:

- ¼ pound sliced fresh mushrooms
- 1/8 teaspoon salt
- ½ small red onion, halved and thinly sliced
- 1/8 teaspoon pepper
- ½ pound fresh green beans, make 2 inch pieces

- 1 tablespoons olive oil
- ½ teaspoon Italian seasoning

Directions:

1. Preheat your air fryer to 375°F.

2. In a large bowl, mix all ingredients together; season with salt and pepper.

3. Arrange vegetables on a greased tray in the air fryer basket, and cook for 8-10 minutes until just tender.

4. Toss to redistribute; cook for an additional 8-10 minutes until browned.

Per serving: Calories: 76 Kcal; Fat: 5 g; Carbs: 8 g; Protein: 3 g; Sugar: 3 g; Sodium: 105 mg

23. Bacon Wrapped Avocado Wedges

Preparation time: 30 minutes

Cooking time: 30 minutes

Servings: 1 Dozen

Ingredients:

- 12 bacon strips
- 2 medium ripe avocados

Sauce

- 1/2 cup mayonnaise
- 1 to 2 tablespoons lime juice
- 2 to 3 tablespoons Sriracha chili sauce
- 1 teaspoon grated lime zest

Directions:

1. Preheat your air fryer to 400°F.

2. To prepare the avocado, remove the pit and peel it.

3. Cut each half into thirds. Wrap 1 slice of bacon around each avocado wedge.

4. Working in batches if needed, place the wedges in a single layer on your tray in the basket of air fryer and then cook until the bacon is cooked for

10-15 minutes. Meanwhile, stir together mayonnaise, Sirach sauce, lime juice, and zest. Serve them up with the sauce on the side!

Per serving: Calories: 114 Kcal; Fat: 2 g; Carbs: 18 g; Protein: 6 g; Sugar: 3 g; Sodium: 338 mg

24. Sweet Potato

Preparation time: 15 minutes

Cooking time: 10 minutes

Servings: 2

Ingredients:

- ½ cup sweet potato chips
- Cooking spray
- 1/8 cup all-purpose flour
- ½ pound chicken tenderloins, cut into 1-1/2-inch pieces
- ½ teaspoon salt, divided
- ½ tablespoon cornstarch
- ¼ teaspoon coarsely ground pepper
- 1/8 teaspoon baking powder

Directions:

1. Preheat the air fryer to 400°F.

2. Combine half of the chips with flour, 1/2 teaspoon salt, and pepper in a food processor. Pulse until ground. Transfer to a shallow dish. In a second bowl, combine the remaining chips with baking powder, cornstarch, and salt; toss with chicken.

3. Toss chicken with potato chip mixture; press to coat. Arrange evenly in a single layer on a greased tray in air-fryer basket; spritz with cooking spray.

4. Cook until golden brown, 3-4 minutes.

5. Turn; spritz again with cooking spray and cook until golden brown and no longer pink, 3-4 more minutes.

Per serving: Calories: 190 Kcal; Fat: 4 g; Carbs: 13 g; Protein: 28 g; Sugar: 1 g; Sodium: 690 mg

25. Air-Fryer Asparags

Preparation time: 20 minutes

Cooking time: 4 minutes

Servings: 2

Ingredients:

- ½ pound fresh asparagus, trimmed
- 1/8 cup mayonnaise
- 2 teaspoons olive oil
- Lemon wedges
- 1 teaspoon grated lemon zest
- 1 tablespoon shredded Parmesan cheese
- 1/8 teaspoon seasoned salt
- ½ garlic clove, minced
- ¼ teaspoon pepper

Directions:

1. Preheat the air fryer to 350°F.

2. To cook asparagus in an air fryer, preheat the air fryer to 375°F.

3. In a large mixing bowl, add all the ingredients and mix until combined well.

4. Add asparagus and toss to coat. Working in batches, place asparagus on a greased tray in the air-fryer basket.

5. Cook until tender and lightly browned, 4–6 minutes. Now transfer this to a platter and sprinkle with some Parmesan cheese. If desired, serve with lemon wedges.

Per serving: Calories: 156 Kcal; Fat: 15 g; Carbs: 3 g; Protein: 2 g; Sugar: 1 g; Sodium: 214 mg

26. Herb and Lemon Cauliflower

Preparation time: 20 minutes

Cooking time: 5 minutes

Servings: 2

Ingredients:

- 1 tablespoon lemon juice
- 2 tablespoons olive oil, divided
- 1/8 teaspoon crushed red pepper flakes
- 1/8 cup minced fresh parsley

- ½ medium head cauliflower, cut into florets
- ½ tablespoon minced fresh rosemary
- 1/4 teaspoon salt
- ½ tablespoon minced fresh thyme
- ½ teaspoon grated lemon zest

Directions:

1. Take a large bowl and add the cauliflower florets to the bowl. Drizzle it with olive oil to make sure the cauliflower is coated well.

2. Arrange the cauliflower on the tray in a Pre-heated air fryer basket. Place them in a single layer so that they can cook evenly.

3. Cook until they are tender and edges are browned, 8-10 minutes, stirring halfway through.

4. In a small bowl, combine the remaining ingredients and toss with the remaining 2 tablespoons olive oil.

5. Dish the cauliflower in a large mixing bowl; drizzle with the herb mixture and toss to combine.

Per serving: Calories: 161 Kcal; Fat: 14 g; Carbs: 8 g; Protein: 3 g; Sugar: 3 g; Sodium: 342 mg

27. **Okra with Smoked Paprika**

Preparation time: 10 minutes

Cooking time: 10 minutes

Servings: 2

Ingredients:

- 1/8 teaspoon salt
- 1/2 pound fresh okra pods
- 1/8 teaspoon pepper
- ½ tablespoon olive oil
- 1/8 teaspoon garlic powder
- ½ tablespoon lemon juice
- 1/4 teaspoon smoked paprika

Directions:

1. Preheat the air fryer to 375°F. Add all the ingredients into a bowl and mix them until they are combined, then spread evenly onto a greased tray. Put the okra in the air fryer basket and cook

until tender and lightly browned, 15-20 minutes, stirring occasionally.

Per serving: Calories: 57 Kcal; Fat: 4 g; Carbs: 6 g; Protein: 2 g; Sugar: 3 g; Sodium: 155 mg

28. **Breaded Summer Squash**

Preparation time: 15 minutes

Cooking time: 10 minutes

Servings: 2

Ingredients:

- 2/4 cup grated Parmesan cheese
- 2 tablespoons olive oil
- 2 cups thinly sliced yellow summer squash
- 1/4 teaspoon salt
- 2/4 cup panko bread crumbs
- 1/4 teaspoon pepper
- 1/8 teaspoon cayenne pepper

Directions:

1. Preheat the air fryer to 350°F.

2. In a large bowl, mix the squash and oil; season with your favorite seasoning. Coat both sides of the squash in bread crumbs and cheese; pat to help the coating adhere. Arrange slices of squash in a single layer on a tray in your air fryer basket.

3. Cook until the squash is tender and golden brown, about 10 minutes.

Per serving: Calories: 203 Kcal; Fat: 14 g; Carbs: 13 g; Protein: 6 g; Sugar: 4 g; Sodium: 554 mg

29. **Air-Fryer Tofu**

Preparation time: 10 minutes

Cooking time: 10 minutes

Servings: 2

Ingredients:

- 7 ounces firm tofu
- 1/8 cup olive oil
- 1 garlic clove, minced
- 1/8 teaspoon crushed red pepper flakes
- 2 tablespoons reduced-sodium soy sauce

- 1/8 teaspoon ground cumin
- 1 green onion, chopped

Directions:

1. To make the tofu, cut the tofu in half lengthwise and then cut each piece in half diagonally to create triangles.

2. Cover with marinade made with remaining ingredients, and let sit at room temperature for 3-5 hours. Heat air fryer to 400°F; place tofu on a greased tray.

3. Drizzle remaining marinade over top of tofu before cooking in air fryer until lightly browned and heated through, 6-8 minutes.

Per serving: Calories: 208 Kcal; Fat: 18 g; Carbs: 4 g; Protein: 4 g; Sugar: 1 g; Sodium: 440 mg

30. Radishes

Preparation time: 15 minutes

Cooking time: 10 minutes

Servings: 4

Ingredients:

- 1/8 teaspoon pepper
- ½ tablespoon minced fresh oregano
- 1/4 pounds radishes, trimmed and quartered
- 1/8 teaspoon salt
- 2 tablespoons olive oil

Directions:

1. To make the radishes, preheat your air fryer to 375°F.

2. Toss the radishes with all other ingredients until coated. Grease the tray, put the radishes on it, and cook until crisp-tender, about 12-15 minutes, stirring occasionally.

Per serving: Calories: 88 Kcal; Fat: 7 g; Carbs: 6 g; Protein: 1 g; Sugar: 3 g; Sodium: 165 mg

31. Red Potatoes

Preparation time: 10 minutes

Cooking time: 10 minutes

Servings: 4

Ingredients:

- 1/8 teaspoon pepper
- 1 pound small red potatoes, cut into wedges
- 1/4 teaspoon salt
- ½ tablespoon minced fresh rosemary
- 1 garlic clove
- 1 tablespoon olive oil

Directions:

1. Preheat the air fryer to 400°F. Drizzle potatoes with oil and then sprinkle them with rosemary, garlic, salt, and pepper; toss gently to coat.

2. Place on an ungreased tray in the air fryer basket. Cook the potatoes until they are golden brown and tender, about 10-12 minutes; stir once during cooking.

Per serving: Calories: 113mKcal; Fat: 4 g; Carbs: 18 g; Protein: 2 g; Sugar: 1 g; Sodium: 155 mg

32. Garlic-Rosemary Brussels Sprouts

Preparation time: 15 minutes

Cooking time: 15 minutes

Servings: 2

Ingredients:

- 1/8 teaspoon pepper
- 2 tablespoons olive oil
- 1/2 teaspoons minced fresh rosemary
- 1/2 pound Brussels sprouts
- 1 garlic clove
- 1/4 teaspoon salt
- 1/4 cup panko bread crumbs

Directions:

1. Preheat the air fryer to 350°F. Put all the ingredients except the bread crumbs in a small microwave-safe bowl; microwave on high for 30 seconds. Toss the Brussels sprouts with 2 tablespoons of oil mixture and place them in an air-fryer basket.

2. Cook them for 4-5 minutes, stirring halfway through cooking time.

3. Stir the Brussels sprouts after they have browned so you get lots of brown spots on them.

4. Cook for about 8 minutes longer, stirring halfway through cooking time.

5. Once they are tender, toss them with some bread crumbs and rosemary oil, then cook until all sides are crispy enough to eat and have golden brown color!

Per serving: Calories: 164 Kcal; Fat: 11 g; Carbs: 15 g; Protein: 5 g; Sugar: 3 g; Sodium: 343 mg

33. **Sweet Potato Nachos**

Preparation time: 12 minutes

Cooking time: 22 minutes

Servings: 2

Ingredients:

- ½ medium sweet potato
- Nonstick cooking spray
- ½ cup frozen pepper-and-onion blend
- ½ jalapeño pepper
- 1/8 cup shredded cheddar
- 1/8 cup salsa
- 2/3 cup thinly sliced radishes
- 2 cherry tomatoes
- ¼ cup shredded lettuce
- 1 tablespoon sour cream
- ½ tablespoon minced fresh cilantro

Directions:

1. Add the sweet potato slices to the air fryer and spray them with a bit of nonstick cooking spray.

2. Spoon the frozen vegetables over the potatoes. Place a jalapeño pepper on top of the vegetables and then spray with nonstick cooking spray for 1 second.

3. Set the temperature of the air fryer to 375° F, and air fry for 20 minutes or until cooked through (they should be tender but crisp).

4. Remove the jalapeño pepper, cover it loosely with a kitchen towel, let stand for 5 minutes, then sprinkle cheese evenly over everything.

5. Remove the charred skin from the jalapeño pepper and finely chop it. Serve with salsa, radishes, tomatoes, and sour cream.

6. **Per serving:** Calories: 100 Kcal; Fat: 2.5 g; Carbs: 17 g; Protein: 4 g; Sugar: 6 g; Sodium: 180 mg

34. **Spicy Green Beans**

Preparation time: 10 minutes

Cooking time: 10 minutes

Servings: 2

Ingredients:

- 6 ounces green beans
- 1 tablespoon olive oil
- ½ teaspoon chili garlic paste
- ½ tablespoon panko bread crumbs
- 1/8 teaspoon salt

Directions:

1. In a small mixing bowl, add olive oil, chili garlic paste, and panko bread crumbs and mix them. Add salt to taste. And toss green beans in it.

2. Place the green beans in a mesh basket and place it inside the air fryer.

3. Set temperature to 400° F and cook for 4 minutes.

4. Shake basket after 4 minutes; continue to cook for 5 to 7 more minutes or until desired doneness is achieved.

5. Serve warm.

Per serving: Calories: 60 Kcal; Fat: 3.5 g; Carbs: 7 g; Protein: 2 g; Sugar: 1 g; Sodium: 160 mg

35. **Fried Avocado Tacos**

Preparation time: 30 minutes

Cooking time: 10 minutes

Servings: 4

Ingredients:

- 2 Cups shredded coleslaw mix
- ¼ Teaspoon pepper
- ¼ Teaspoon salt
- ¼ Cup minced cilantro

- 1 Teaspoon honey
- ¼ Cup Greek yogurt
- 2 Tablespoons lime juice

For Tacos

- 1 Egg
- 1 Medium tomato
- ¼ Cup cornmeal
- 8 flour tortillas
- 2 Medium avocado
- ½ Teaspoon garlic powder
- Salt and pepper

Directions:

1. To make the kale mix, combine the first 8 ingredients in a bowl. Refrigerate, covered, until serving.

2. To make the salad, place avocado slices in a shallow bowl. Take another large and shallow bowl, mix cornmeal, salt, garlic powder and chipotle pepper.

3. Dip the avocado slices in egg, then into the cornmeal mixture; pat gently to help adhere.

4. In batches, place avocado slices in a single layer on greased tray in air fryer basket; spritz with cooking spray.

5. Cook until golden brown for 3-4 minutes or until cooked and crispy on both sides. Turn; spritz with cooking spray again if necessary.

6. Cook until golden brown for another 4-5 minutes or until cooked through and crispy on both sides. Serve with salad greens and salsa Verde (optional).

Per serving: Calories: 407Kcal; Fat: 21g; Carbs: 48g; Protein: 9g; Sugar: 4g; Sodium: 738mg

36. Buffalo Bites

Preparation time: 10 minutes

Cooking time: 30 minutes

Servings: 6

Ingredients:

- 1 Small cauliflower head
- 3 Tablespoons melted butter
- 2 Tablespoons olive oil
- 1 ½ Cups cottage cheese
- ¼ Cup crumbled blue cheese
- 3 Tablespoons buffalo wing sauce
- ¼ Cup Greek yogurt
- 1 Envelope ranch salad dressing

Directions:

1. Preheat air fryer to 350°F.

2. In a large bowl, combine Buffalo sauce and melted butter; mix well.

3. Add cauliflower; toss to coat. Arrange in single layer in air-fryer basket.

4. Cook until florets are tender and edges are browned, 10-15 minutes, stirring halfway through cooking time.

Per serving: Calories: 203Kcal; Fat: 13g; Carbs: 13g; Protein: 8g; Sugar: 4g; Sodium: 1470mg

37. Portobello Melts

Preparation time: 25 minutes

Cooking time: 10-15 minutes

Servings: 2

Ingredients:

- 2 Portobello mushrooms
- 2 Tablespoons balsamic vinegar
- 4 Tomato Slices
- Chopped Fresh basil
- ½ Teaspoon Dried basil
- 2 Slices mozzarella cheese
- ¼ Cup olive oil
- Salt
- Italian bread (2 Slices)

Directions:

1. In a bowl, mix oil, vinegar, salt, and dried basil.

2. Brush both sides of the mushrooms with this mixture. Let stand for 5 minutes. Reserve the remaining marinade for another use.

3. Set the temperature to 400 °F of your air fryer.

4. Place mushrooms on a greased tray in an air fryer basket and top them with tomato and cheese; secure them with toothpicks.

5. Cook until the cheese is melted, about one minute per side.

6. Remove from basket and keep warm while you make the toastables; discard the toothpicks once they cool off a bit.

7. Place bread slices in the basket of an air fryer. Brush with reserved marinade. Cook until lightly toasted, 2-3 minutes. Top with mushrooms and chopped basil.

Per serving: Calories: 427Kcal; Fat: 30g; Carbs: 33g; Protein: 8g; Sugar: 8g; Sodium: 864mg

38. Acorn Squash Slices

Preparation time: 15 minutes

Cooking time: 15 minutes

Servings: 6

Ingredients:

- ½ Cup Butter
- 2 Acorn squash
- 2/3 Cup brown sugar

Directions:

1. Preheat the air fryer to 350°F.

2. Cut squash in half lengthwise, remove and discard the seeds, and then cut each half crosswise into half-inch slices.

3. Arrange the squash on a greased tray in the air fryer basket; cook until tender, about 5 minutes per side.

4. Meanwhile, combine sugar and butter; spread over the squash and cook for 3 minutes longer.

Per serving: Calories: 320Kcal; Fat: 16g; Carbs: 48g; Protein: 2g; Sugar: 29g; Sodium: 135mg

39. Green Tomato Stacks

Preparation time: 20 minutes

Cooking time: 15 minutes

Servings: 6

Ingredients:

- 8 slices Canadian bacon
- 2 medium red tomatoes
- 1/4 teaspoon salt
- 2 large egg whites
- 1/2 teaspoon pepper
- 2 tablespoons lime juice
- 1/4 cup fat-free mayonnaise
- 1/4 teaspoon grated lime zest
- 1 teaspoon minced fresh thyme
- 1/4 cup all-purpose flour
- 3/4 cup cornmeal
- 2 medium green tomatoes
- Cooking spray

Directions:

1. For this recipe, preheat your air fryer to 375°F.

2. Combine 1/4 teaspoon pepper, lime zest and juice, thyme and mayonnaise; refrigerate for up to 1 hour before serving.

3. To make the cornmeal mixture, mix 1/2 tablespoon of cornmeal with 1/4 teaspoon of salt and pepper.

4. Coat 4 slices of green tomato in the cornmeal mixture one by one then dip it in egg whites before putting it in the air fryer basket.

5. Turn once after half a minute and repeat until all the slices are browned.

6. For each serving, stack 1 slice of bacon, green and red tomatoes together on a plate and serve with sauce on top.

Per serving: Calories: 114Kcal; Fat: 2g; Carbs: 18g; Protein: 6g; Sugar: 3g; Sodium: 338mg

40. Pepper Poppers

Preparation time: 20 minutes

Cooking time: 15 minutes

Servings: 2 Dozen

Ingredients:

- 1 package cream cheese
- 3/4 cup shredded Monterey Jack cheese
- 1/4 teaspoon salt
- 1/4 teaspoon chili powder
- 1 pound fresh jalapenos
- Sour cream
- 1/2 cup dry bread crumbs
- 1/4 teaspoon smoked paprika
- 1/4 teaspoon garlic powder
- 6 bacon strips, cooked and crumbled
- 3/4 cup shredded cheddar cheese

Directions:

1. Preheat your air fryer to 325°F.

2. Take a large bowl, and add the cheeses, bacon, and seasonings; mix well.

3. Spoon 1-1/2 to 2 tablespoons of the mixture into each pepper half.

4. Roll in bread crumbs. Spritz the basket with cooking spray, working in batches if needed.

5. Place poppers in the basket, then cook until cheese is melted and heated through, 15-20 minutes.

6. Serve with sour cream or dip if desired!

Per serving: Calories: 81Kcal; Fat: 6g; Carbs: 3g; Protein: 3g; Sugar: 1g; Sodium: 145mg

CHAPTER 3: Beans and Grains

41. Green Beans

Preparation time: 2 minutes

Cooking time: 6 minutes

Servings: 4

Ingredients:

- 1pound green beans
- cooking spray
- salt to taste

Directions:

1. First, preheat the air fryer to 400 °F.

2. Spray the green beans with a little low-calorie spray, then sprinkle with sea salt and freshly ground black pepper.

3. Gently mix the ingredients with your hands and place them in the air fryer basket.

4. Cook for 6-8 minutes, turning them occasionally so they brown evenly.

5. Remove from heat and serve topped with extra salt and chopped herbs if you like.

Per serving: Calories: 35Kcal; Fat: 5g; Carbs: 7g; Protein: 2g; Sugar: 3g; Sodium: 6mg

42. Garlic Butter Sesame Green Beans

Preparation time: 5 minutes

Cooking time: 5 minutes

Servings: 8

Ingredients:

- 1 pound green beans topped and tailed
- 1 teaspoon garlic purée
- ½ teaspoon sesame oil
- 1 cup chicken stock
- 1 tablespoon butter
- 1 tablespoon toasted sesame seeds

Directions:

1. Add chicken stock to a saucepan.

2. Then add the green beans, butter, and garlic.

3. Cook it for 5 minutes or until the stock is reduced to half.

4. Set the air-fryer to 350 °F.

5. Remove the beans from the saucepan, place them on the basket, and cook for another 5 minutes.

6. Top with sesame seeds and serve immediately.

Per serving: Calories: 68Kcal; Fat: 4g; Carbs: 7g; Protein: 3g; Sugar: 3g; Sodium: 79mg

43. Smothered Green Beans

Preparation time: 10 minutes

Cooking time: 25 minutes

Servings: 6

Ingredients:

- 2 teaspoons vegetable oil
- 1 pound green beans washed and trimmed
- 8 slices cooked bacon cut or crumbled
- 6 small shallots
- one small onion
- garlic salt
- 1 cup chicken stock

Directions:

1. Sauté the shallots in a large skillet over medium heat for a few minutes until they turn light brown.

2. Add a third of the bacon and fresh green beans, then cook for 1 minute in an air fryer.

3. Add garlic salt, chicken stock and stir occasionally for about 15 minutes or until fork tender.

4. Serve and enjoy.

Per serving: Calories: 68Kcal; Fat: 2g; Carbs: 11g; Protein: 3g; Sugar: 5g; Sodium: 67mg

44. Asian Sesame Green Beans

Preparation time: 2 minutes

Cooking time: 8 minutes

Servings: 4

Ingredients:

- 12 ounces fresh green beans, trimmed
- 1 tablespoon soy sauce
- Salt and pepper, to taste
- 4 teaspoons sesame oil
- 1 teaspoon Sriracha sauce
- 1-2 teaspoons sesame seeds

Directions:

1. To make Asian sesame green beans, preheat the air fryer to 375 °F.

2. Take a large mixing bowl, toss the green beans with 1 teaspoon of sesame oil.

3. Work in batches if you can; cook the beans in the air fryer basket, tossing once halfway through cooking.

4. While the beans are cooking, whisk the remaining sesame oil, soy sauce, and Sriracha sauce until smooth.

5. Finally, transfer the green beans to a bowl and toss with sauce before serving.

Per serving: Calories: 60Kcal; Fat: 4g; Carbs: 7g; Protein: 2g; Sugar: 3g; Sodium: 150mg

45. Kidney Bean Popcorn

Preparation time: 5 minutes

Cooking time: 25 minutes

Servings: 2

Ingredients:

- 1can kidney beans
- olive oil cooking spray
- 1 teaspoon sea salt

Directions:

1. To make Air-fried kidney beans, preheat an air fryer to 325 °F (165 °C).

2. Then use olive oil to spray kidney beans and toss with sea salt.

3. Spread them out in a single layer in the air fryer basket, then air-fry until you see that all kidney beans have split open and become crispy, 25 to 30 minutes.

4. If they look under-toasted, fry for another 5 minutes; they would have varying degrees of brown.

5. Now let it cool down for a while and store in an airtight container.

Per serving: Calories: 178Kcal; Fat: 0.8g; Carbs: 32g; Protein: 11.3g; Sugar: 0g; Sodium: 1332mg

46. Red Kidney Beans Pakora

Preparation time: 5 minutes

Cooking time: 14 minutes

Servings: 15

Ingredients:

- 1/2 Cup Red Kidney Beans
- 1/2 Cup Yellow Moong dal
- Finely chopped cabbage
- Onions
- Green chilies
- Small piece of ginger (Chopped)
- Finely chopped coriander
- Tablespoon Oil
- Salt
- Sweet Mango Chutney

Directions:

1. In a large bowl, combine red kidney beans, yellow moong dal, salt, and green chilies, soak them overnight, then grind.

2. Pour the mixture into a bowl, then add vegetables.

3. Taste for salt and add accordingly.

4. Grease the Air-fryer basket with oil.

5. Place 5 batter balls in each section of the basket. Press with fingers on each one to ensure even compression.

6. Spray oil over each section of the basket before closing it.

7. Bake for 14 minutes and make sure it has a golden brown top.

8. Serve with sweet mango chutney or tomato rasam sauce.

Per serving: Calories: 188Kcal; Fat: 2g; Carbs: 41g; Protein: 4g; Sugar: 3g; Sodium: 1015mg

47. Baked Beans

Preparation time: 5 minutes

Cooking time: 12 minutes

Servings: 4

Ingredients:

- 28 ounces baked beans
- 4 tablespoons brown sugar
- 3 tablespoons ketchup
- 2 tablespoons yellow mustard
- Bacon strips

Directions:

1. Spread the beans out on an air fryer safe pan.

2. Next, add the brown sugar, ketchup, and yellow mustard. Mix well until combined, then add your bacon strips to the beans.

3. Set the temperature on your air fryer to 400 °F for 12 minutes.

4. Plate and serve!

Per serving: Calories: 119Kcal; Fat: 0.5g; Carbs: 27g; Protein: 6g; Sugar: 0g; Sodium: 430mg

48. Green Sauce and Pinto Beans Queso

Preparation time: 5 minutes

Cooking time: 15 minutes

Servings: 10

Ingredients:

- 32 Oz Easy Melt Cheese
- 1 cup canned pinto beans
- 11 Oz Green Sauce Medium

Directions:

5. To make this dish, place pinto beans, cheese and sauce into an air fryer pan.

6. Cook at 350°F for 15 minutes, Stir it occasionally.

7. You can serve it with chips, or it can be used as topping for burritos or quesadillas.

Per serving: Calories: 340Kcal; Fat: 24g; Carbs: 14g; Protein: 17g; Sugar: 7g; Sodium: 1790mg

49. Crispy Black-Eyed Peas

Preparation time: 5 minutes

Cooking time: 10 minutes

Servings: 6

Ingredients:

- 1 15- ounce can black-eyed peas
- 1/4 teaspoon salt
- 1/8 teaspoon black pepper
- 1/2 teaspoon chili powder
- 1/8 teaspoon chipotle chili powder
- 1/8 teaspoon smoked salt

Directions:

1. To make delicious black-eyed peas, drain the liquid from black-eyed peas. In the running water wash them and let them drain.

2. Spread them out on a plate and remove all the mushy peas.

3. Take a small bowl, mix all the ingredients, and sprinkle as much as you want according to your taste, gently stirring the peas to ensure all are coated.

4. Place the peas in your air fryer at 350-360 °F.

5. Cook the peas for about 5 minutes, then take them out from the basket and shake or stir to redistribute the peas.

6. Return to the basket and cook for another 5 minutes or until peas are crunchy on the outside and tender on the inside.

7. Allow to cool before serving.

Per serving: Calories: 82Kcal; Fat: 0.28g; Carbs: 14g; Protein: 2.48g; Sugar: 2.34g; Sodium: 266mg

50. Chick-Peas with Za'atar

Preparation time: 2 minutes

Cooking time: 18 minutes

Servings: 8

Ingredients:

- 4 Tablespoon Olive Oil
- 1 can Canned Chickpeas
- 4 Tablespoon za'atar
- Salt

Directions:

1. Drain excess liquid and rinse chickpeas thoroughly.

2. Add chickpeas to a large mixing bowl, drizzle them with olive oil, and add some salt and za'atar blend according to your liking.

3. Heat air fryer for 18 minutes, tossing twice during the cooking cycle.

4. Serve hot with tortilla chips or on top of salads.

Per serving: Calories: 117Kcal; Fat: 8g; Carbs: 9g; Protein: 3g; Sugar: 1g; Sodium: mg

51. Jamaican Peas and Rice

Preparation time: 5 minutes

Cooking time: 10 minutes

Servings: 4

Ingredients:

- 1 cup Jasmine Rice
- 1 cup Water
- 1 tablespoon vegetable oil
- 1 Scotch Bonnet Pepper
- 3 sprigs Dried Thyme
- 1 teaspoon Kosher Salt

- 1/2 teaspoon Ground Allspice
- 1 cup canned kidney beans
- 1/2 cup Full-Fat Coconut Milk

Directions:

1. Place the rice into pot filled with water and boil them for about 8-9 mins. Don't forget to rinse and drain them in the first place.

2. Add the scotch bonnet pepper, thyme, salt, allspice, and water and mix well.

3. Pour in the vegetable oil and stir lightly.

4. Add the kidney beans to the pot.

5. Drain the water and place the rice-beans in air fryer.

6. Cook at high temperature for 4 minutes.

7. Add coconut milk, mix well, and put them again in the air fryer. Let the rice and beans absorb coconut milk.

8. Serve and Enjoy.

Per serving: Calories: 262Kcal; Fat: 6g; Carbs: 44g; Protein: 5g; Sugar: 1g; Sodium: 778mg

52. Cranberry Beans

Preparation time: 20 minutes

Cooking time: 60 minutes

Servings: 8

Ingredients:

For Brine:

- 1 lb dried cranberry beans
- Water
- 1 Tablespoon salt

For Cook:

- 3 cups broth vegetable
- 3 cups water
- 1 Teaspoon cumin-coriander mix
- ¼ cup red chile sauce
- Salt, to taste
- Pepper, to taste

Directions:

1. Mix 1 tablespoon of salt and 1 cup of water in a large bowl. Pour the mixture over the dried beans and stir until the salt dissolves. Let them soak for 4 hours.

2. Rinse the beans, then add them to an air fryer with broth and water.

3. Add cumin, coriander seeds, and red chilies.

4. Set the air fryer to medium heat and bring it to a boil.

5. Reduce to a simmer and cover. Cook for 1-1/2 hours, stirring frequently until the beans are tender. If they start sticking or the water drops below the surface of the beans, add more liquid—just enough so that they will float on top rather than sit on their own at the bottom.

Per serving: Calories: 194Kcal; Fat: 1g; Carbs: 35g; Protein: 13g; Sugar: 1g; Sodium: 1232mg

53. Crispy Roasted Lentils

Preparation time: 5 minutes

Cooking time: 20 minutes

Servings: 4

Ingredients:

- 2 cups cooked lentils canned
- 2 tablespoons olive oil
- 1 teaspoon chipotle paste

Directions:

1. Set up the heat of the air fryer to 400° F.

2. Combine lentils with oil and chipotle and toss gently to combine.

3. Spread on a small sheet of aluminum foil and fold up the sides of the foil to create a tray.

4. Cook until lightly crisp, about 15 minutes, stirring halfway through.

Per serving: Calories: 178Kcal; Fat: 7g; Carbs: 20g; Protein: 9g; Sugar: 2g; Sodium: 18mg

54. Spicy Green Beans

Preparation time: 10 minutes

Cooking time: 25 minutes

Servings: 4

Ingredients:

- 12 ounces fresh green beans
- 1 teaspoon soy sauce
- 1 clove garlic, minced
- 1 tablespoon sesame oil
- 1 teaspoon rice wine vinegar
- ½ teaspoon red pepper flakes

Directions:

1. Preheat air fryer to 400 °F.

2. Place green beans in a bowl, and then whisk together sesame oil, soy sauce, rice wine vinegar, and red pepper flakes.

3. Pour over green beans and toss to coat.

4. Let marinate for 5 minutes before you cook them in the air fryer.

Per serving: Calories: 59Kcal; Fat: 3.6g; Carbs: 6.6g; Protein: 1.7g; Sugar: 1.3g; Sodium: 80mg

55. Green Beans and Potato Fry

Preparation time: 10 minutes

Cooking time: 12 minutes

Servings: 2

Ingredients:

- 1 Cup Potato cubes
- 1 Small Chopped Onion
- 1 Teaspoon Coriander powder
- ¼ Teaspoon Garam masala Powder
- ½ Teaspoon Ginger Garlic Paste
- 1 Teaspoon Lime juice
- 1.5 Cups Chopped Green Beans
- ½ Teaspoon Turmeric Powder
- ½ Teaspoon Red Chili Powder
- Salt to taste
- 1 Teaspoon Oil

Directions:

1. Wash the vegetables in running water and cut them. Mix all the vegetables with all the spices and oil in a large bowl.

2. Put parchment paper on the air fryer basket as a lining.

3. Arrange the vegetables on top of the parchment paper so that they won't burn.

4. Then put them in your air fryer and cook for about 10-12 minutes, until done.

5. Stir them occasionally to make sure even cooking. It should turn to a golden brown color when done cooking.

6. Remove them from the air fryer when they are done; sprinkle some lime juice over the top and garnish with cilantro leaves (optional).

7. Enjoy them with some dinner!

Per serving: Calories: 80Kcal; Fat: 2g; Carbs: 14g; Protein: 4g; Sugar: 7g; Sodium: 10mg

56. Garlic Green Beans with Lemon

Preparation time: 5 minutes

Cooking time: 8 minutes

Servings: 4

Ingredients:

- 1 pound green beans
- ½ teaspoon salt
- 1 teaspoon garlic powder
- grated parmesan cheese
- lemon wedges to serve
- 1 tablespoon lemon juice
- ½ teaspoon ground black pepper
- 1 tablespoon olive oi

Directions:

1. To wash and dry green beans, put them in a colander and rinse under warm water.

2. Trim the ends, spray with olive oil, season with salt, black pepper, and garlic powder (or other spices), then toss to coat.

3. Add lemon juice while they're still wet; they need to be firm enough to hold their shape when cooked.

4. Preheat the Air fryer and set the temperature to 400°F; place the green beans in a basket, and cook for 6-8 minutes without shaking.

5. Transfer from your Air fryer, plate up with melted parmesan cheese and lemon wedges for presentation if you like.

Per serving: Calories: 68Kcal; Fat: 4g; Carbs: 8g; Protein: 2g; Sugar: 4g; Sodium: 298mg

57. Crispy Fried Green Beans

Preparation time: 10 minutes

Cooking time: 10 minutes

Servings:

Ingredients:

- 1 pound fresh green beans
- 3-4 large eggs
- 1 teaspoon salt
- 1 cup all-purpose flour
- 2 cups Italian seasoned bread crumbs
- 1 teaspoon pepper

Directions:

1. To make air-fried green beans, wash and trim the beans, then let them dry completely.

2. Spread them out on a large baking sheet and spray with a light layer of cooking spray.

3. In a bowl, combine flour, eggs, seasoned bread crumbs, and salt & pepper.

4. Dip each bean into the flour to coat, then into the beaten eggs, and finally into the seasoned bread crumbs.

5. Working in batches, place beans in your air fryer basket so they are in a single layer.

6. Air fry at 375° F for 5-7 minutes or until golden brown and crispy.

7. Remove from the basket and serve them hot.

Per serving: Calories: 226Kcal; Fat: 4g; Carbs: 37g; Protein: 10g; Sugar: 4g; Sodium: 704mg

58. Easy Green Beans with Bacon

Preparation time: 5 minutes

Cooking time: 10 minutes

Servings: 4

Ingredients:

- 1 pound washed green beans
- ¼ cup yellow onion chopped
- ½ teaspoon salt
- 1 teaspoon garlic powder
- ½ teaspoon ground black pepper
- 2 tablespoons olive oil
- 3 slices bacon cut into ½ inch pieces

Directions:

1. To make green beans with bacon, wash and trim the beans if necessary.

2. Then chop the yellow onion.

3. Finally, cut the bacon into thin strips.

4. Mix green beans, olive oil, salt, and pepper in a medium bowl. Stir until well-coated with oil.

5. Add green beans to air fryer basket and top with onion and bacon. Make sure onions and bacon are evenly distributed over the green beans.

6. Air fry at 370 °F for 10-12 minutes until bacon is crispy and green beans are slightly browned from the heat generated by cooking in an air-filled cavity.

7. Remove from air fryer and serve with fresh lemon juice squeezed on top!

Per serving: Calories: 173Kcal; Fat: 14g; Carbs: 10g; Protein: 4g; Sugar: 4g; Sodium: 408mg

59. Baked Beans

Preparation time: 5 minutes

Cooking time: 12 minutes

Servings: 4

Ingredients:

- 28 ounces baked beans
- 4 tablespoons brown sugar

- 3 tablespoons ketchup
- 2 tablespoons yellow mustard

Directions:

1. Start by spreading your beans out in an air fryer safe pan.

2. Then add the brown sugar, ketchup, and mustard. Mix well, make sure everything is combined and place your bacon strips directly on top of the beans.

3. Set it in your air fryer basket for 12 minutes at 400°F.

4. Dish out on a platter and serve.

Per serving: Calories: 119Kcal; Fat: 0.5g; Carbs 27g; Protein: 6g; Sugar: 4g; Sodium: 778mg

60. Chinese Beef with Green Beans

Preparation time: 30 minutes

Cooking time: 10 minutes

Servings: 2

Ingredients:

- 1/2 pound Flank steak
- 1 teaspoon Oyster sauce
- 1/4 teaspoon Baking soda
- 1 tablespoon Water
- 1 teaspoon Cornstarch
- 1 tablespoon Vegetable oil

Sauce:

- 1 tablespoon Hoisin sauce
- 1 tablespoon Water
- 1 teaspoon Fresh ginger,
- 1 tablespoon Oyster sauce
- 1/2 teaspoon Toasted sesame oil
- 2 cloves Garlic, minced

Green Beans:

- 1/2 pound Green beans, stem ends trimmed
- Toasted sesame seeds, for garnish
- Sliced scallions, for garnish
- Hot rice, for serving

Directions:

1. Slice the beef 1/4 inch thick. Combine it with water, oyster sauce, cornstarch, and baking soda in a bowl.

2. Mix until it is evenly coated.

3. Let it marinate for 20 to 30 minutes and preheat an air fryer to 400°F.

4. To make sauce: Mix hoisin sauce, oyster sauce, water, sesame oil, ginger, and garlic in a large bowl.

5. Add marinated beef and green beans; gently stir to coat.

6. Spread out in air fryer basket; cook until green beans are crisp-tender and meat is crisp at edge; open halfway through cooking time

Per serving: Calories: 318Kcal; Fat: 10.6g; Carbs: 22g; Protein: 36.6g; Sugar: 1.8g; Sodium: 489mg

61. Green Beans with Gremolata and Toasted Almonds

Preparation time: 10 minutes

Cooking time: 10 minutes

Servings: 4

Ingredients:

- 1 pound green beans
- Kosher salt
- ground black pepper
- 1 small clove garlic
- Finely grated zest from 1/2 lemon
- 3 tablespoons roasted sliced almonds
- 4 cup roughly chopped fresh parsley
- 1 tablespoon olive oil

Directions:

1. Set the air fryer to 375 °F.

2. In a large bowl, toss the green beans, olive oil, and 1/2 teaspoon salt until evenly combined.

3. Transfer to an air-fryer basket and cook until tender and blistered in spots, about 12 minutes.

4. Meanwhile, stir together the parsley and garlic with lemon zest, 1/8 teaspoon salt, a couple grinds of pepper until combined.

5. Stir in almonds until coated; serve on top of green beans.

Per serving: Calories: 142Kcal; Fat: 11.5g; Carbs: 9g; Protein: 4g; Sugar: 0g; Sodium: 142mg

62. Potatoes with Green Beans

Preparation time: 10 minutes

Cooking time: 25 minutes

Servings: 6

Ingredients:

- 12 Trimmed Green Beans
- 1/2 Teaspoon Garlic Salt
- 2 Tablespoon Shredded Bacon
- 2 Pounds Baby Yellow Gold Potatoes Halved
- Olive Oil Cooking Spray

Directions:

1. Prepare your air fryer and heat it to 390 °F.

2. Place the potatoes and beans in the basket of your air fryer.

3. Top with shredded bacon if preferred.

4. Sprinkle evenly with garlic salt and let them cook for 25 minutes.

5. Check them halfway through the cooking time and stir them occasionally.

6. At this point, add an additional coat of olive oil if needed.

Per serving: Calories: 133Kcal; Fat: 4g; Carbs: 21g; Protein: 5g; Sugar: 3g; Sodium: 220mg

63. Black Eyed Peas

Preparation time: 5 minutes

Cooking time: 15 minutes

Servings: 6

Ingredients:

- 1 can black eyed peas
- Old Bay Seasoning

- Salt
- Canola oil

Directions:

1. Toss one tablespoon of oil into the well of the air fryer.

2. Add Old Bay Seasoning and salt. Stir in black-eyed peas, then place them in the basket.

3. Put it in the air fryer, turn it to 390 °F, and set it for 10 minutes.

4. After 5 minutes, pull out the basket and give it a shake to toss the black-eyed peas around; push it back into the fryer for the remaining time.

5. Taste and add more seasoning as desired.

Per serving: Calories: 54Kcal; Fat: 2g; Carbs: 6g; Protein: 2g; Sugar: 1g; Sodium: 124mg

64. Black Eyed Peas Fritters With Green

Preparation time: 10 minutes

Cooking time: 25 minutes

Servings: 12

Ingredients:

- 3 Teaspoon coriander
- 1/2 tap turmeric
- 3 medium potatoes
- 3 garlic cloves
- 1 cup frozen Black Eyed Peas
- 2 Tablespoon Parsley
- 2 Tablespoon cooking oil
- cooking spray
- salt and pepper to taste
- 1 cup frozen spinach
- 1 inch chunk of fresh ginger
- 1 red onion
- 1 Teaspoon Cayenne
- 2 tap smoked paprika

Directions:

1. First, boil the potatoes. Peel them immediately and then add them to a mixing bowl.

2. Mash them up and set them aside.

3. Then, peel the onion, ginger, and garlic. Chop up these vegetables as small as possible.

4. Add 2 tbsp of cooking oil to a pan and cook over medium heat for 10 minutes.

5. Add in frozen spinach and black-eyed peas and stir well.

6. Then add cayenne, coriander powder (spice mix), smoked paprika, and turmeric powder (color enhancers) into that pan; stir until all spices are incorporated well into the mix.

7. Remove from heat and pour into cooked potatoes; mix well until cool enough to handle.

8. Grab handfuls of mixture up; shape into patties with your hands or on your fingertips; place on an air fryer tray lined with a silpat or parchment paper or on a plate lined with foil before placing in an air fryer

9. Place formed fritters in air-fryer and cook at 425 °F for 10 minutes.

10. Turnover and cook for another 10 minutes.

Per serving: Calories: 181Kcal; Fat: 5g; Carbs: 29g; Protein: 6g; Sugar: 3g; Sodium: 93mg

65. Chinese Style Green Beans

Preparation time: 5 minutes

Cooking time: 15 minutes

Servings: 4

Ingredients:

- 16 fresh green beans
- sesame seeds, for sprinkling
- 1 Tablespoon olive oil

Sauce

- 1/4 cup low sodium soy sauce
- 3 cloves garlic, finely chopped
- 1/4 cup water
- 1 Tablespoon rice wine vinegar
- 2 Tablespoon brown sugar
- 1/2 tsp cornstarch

Directions:

1. You can cook Chinese style green beans on an air fryer. Preheat the air fryer and set the temperature to 375 °F. If it doesn't have a preheat setting, just turn it to 400 °F and give it about 3-5 minutes to come to temperature.

2. In a large bowl, combine olive oil with green beans and spread them onto an air fryer tray or basket.

3. Air fry for 10-12 minutes. Give them a shake about halfway through.

4. While the green beans are cooking, make the sauce by combining all the ingredients of the sauce in a saucepan over medium heat; boil and whisk occasionally for 7-8 minutes until the sauce is thickened; remove green beans from air fryer and put them into a large bowl.

5. Pour sauce over green beans and toss them well before serving immediately so they stay crisp. To add extra flavor, top with sesame seeds if desired before serving.

Per serving: Calories: 92Kcal; Fat: 3.7g; Carbs: 13g; Protein: 2.5g; Sugar: 6.1g; Sodium: 234mg

66. **Roasted Garlic Green Beans**

Preparation time: 5 minutes

Cooking time: 10 minutes

Servings: 4

Ingredients:

- 1 lb. green beans
- 1 tablespoon vegetable oil
- 1 teaspoon Italian seasoning
- 1 teaspoon balsamic vinegar
- ½ teaspoon black pepper
- 1 tablespoon garlic
- 1 teaspoon sesame oil
- 1 teaspoon Worcestershire sauce
- 1 teaspoon soy sauce

Directions:

1. Wash, trim and dry the green beans.

2. Add them to a large mixing bowl, along with all other ingredients. Toss to combine.

3. Transfer the green beans into the air fryer basket and cook at 350 °F for 10 minutes until tender but still crunchy.

4. Shake the basket halfway through cooking.

Per serving: Calories: 83Kcal; Fat: 4.8g; Carbs: 3.8g; Protein: 2.4g; Sugar: 4g; Sodium: 57.7mg

67. **Green Bean Casserole**

Preparation time: 5 minutes

Cooking time: 15 minutes

Servings: 6

Ingredients:

- 14 ounces green beans canned.
- 1 can condensed cream of mushroom soup
- 6 ounces fried onions divided

Directions:

1. Preheat the air fryer by setting its temperature to 350°F.

2. Grease a 6" square baking dish with cooking spray.

3. Take a bowl and mix beans, condensed soup, and half the onions.

4. Pour mixture into the greased baking dish and top with remaining onions.

5. Bake this mixture for 15 minutes or until heated through and onions have browned.

Per serving: Calories: 229Kcal; Fat: 15g; Carbs: 19g; Protein: 4g; Sugar: 2g; Sodium: 601mg

68. **Sichuan-Style Green Beans**

Preparation time: 5 minutes

Cooking time: 10 minutes

Servings: 2

Ingredients:

- 3/4 lb green beans, ends trimmed
- 1/4 Teaspoon salt
- 1 large clove chopped
- 1 Teaspoon chili-garlic sauce

- 1 Teaspoon soy sauce
- 1 Teaspoon ground Sichuan peppercorn
- 2 Teaspoon sesame oil

Directions:

1. Sichuan style green beans are an excellent addition to any meal. To prepare them, remove any damaged florets and trim any excess stem.

2. Preheat your Air Fryer to 400 °F.

3. Add salt, ground Sichuan peppercorn, garlic, and sesame oil to a bowl and gently toss with tongs until all the ingredients are evenly distributed throughout the green beans.

4. Add the seasoned green beans to a plate or basket in your Air Fryer and cook for 6 minutes.

5. Shake well and continue cooking for another 5-6 minutes or until the green beans have blistered and began to char slightly.

6. While they are cooking, mix soy sauce and chili-garlic sauce; add these ingredients to a serving plate along with the cooked green beans that have been placed on top of it.

7. Drizzle each serving with soy chili-garlic sauce before serving. Enjoy!

Per serving: Calories: 80Kcal; Fat: 2.5g; Carbs: 14g; Protein: 4g; Sugar: 7g; Sodium: 10mg

69. Lemon Pepper Green Beans

Preparation time: 15 minutes

Cooking time: 8 minutes

Servings: 4

Ingredients:

- 1 pound green beans
- 1 teaspoon black pepper
- lemon zest of 1 lemon
- 1 Tablespoon vegetable oil
- 1 teaspoon salt
- 2 Tablespoons lemon juice

Directions:

1. To make the lemon pepper green beans, zest the lemon. Take a lemon and cut it in half. Use the half and set one half aside for later use.

2. Trim and clean the beans under running water and then toss them with oil, freshly ground black pepper, salt, and few drops of the lemon juice onto them to coat.

3. Spread out the beans in the air fryer basket and fry at 375°F for 7 minutes, tossing halfway through.

4. Remove from the air fryer with tongs or spatula and sprinkle with remaining lemon juice and zest.

5. Serve warm with pita bread or crackers.

Per serving: Calories: 168Kcal; Fat: 4g; Carbs: 26g; Protein: 12g; Sugar: 12g; Sodium: 2210mg

70. Spicy Asian Green Beans

Preparation time: 15 minutes

Cooking time: 8 minutes

Servings: 4

Ingredients:

- 1 pound green beans
- 1 Tablespoon soy sauce
- ½ teaspoon garlic powder
- 1 teaspoon salt
- 1 Tablespoon vegetable oil
- ½ Tablespoon white wine vinegar
- ¼ teaspoon red pepper flakes
- sesame seeds for finishing

Directions:

1. Trim and clean the beans, toss them with some oil, soy sauce, white wine vinegar, garlic powder, red pepper flakes, and salt.

2. Spread the beans out in a single layer in the air fryer basket.

3. Fry at 375°F for 7 minutes—tossing halfway through.

4. Remove from the air fryer and sprinkle with sesame seeds if desired before serving.

Per serving: Calories: 160Kcal; Fat: 2g; Carbs: 25g;
Protein: 15g; Sugar: 10g; Sodium: 2074mg

CHAPTER 4: Fish and Seafood

71. Crumbed Fish

Preparation time: 10 minutes

Cooking time: 12 minutes

Servings: 4

Ingredients:

- 1 cup dry bread crumbs
- 4 flounder fillets
- 1 lemon, sliced
- ¼ cup vegetable oil
- 1 egg

Directions:

1. To make air fried crumbed fish, preheat an air fryer to 350 °F (180 °C).

2. Mix bread crumbs with oil in a bowl until the mixture becomes loose and crumbly.

3. Dip fish fillets into the egg; and then dip fillets into the bread crumb mixture; coat evenly and fully.

4. Lay coated fillets gently in a preheated air fryer for about 12 minutes or until fish flakes easily with a fork.

5. Garnish with lemon slices.

Per serving: Calories: 304 Kcal; Fat: 9 g; Carbs: 33 g; Protein: 23 g; Sugar: 3 g; Sodium: 503 mg

72. Gingered Honey Salmon

Preparation time: 10 minutes

Cooking time: 15 minutes

Servings: 4

Ingredients:

- 1/2 teaspoon garlic powder
- 1/8 cup honey
- 2/3 cup orange juice
- 1/2 salmon fillet
- 2/3 cup reduced-sodium soy sauce
- ½ green onion, chopped
- 1/2 teaspoon ground ginger

Directions:

1. Mix together the first six ingredients in a shallow bowl and place it in the refrigerator for 30 minutes.

2. Rinse off the salmon, pat dry, then add 2/3 cup of this mixture to the baking pan with the rest of the marinade.

3. Cover with foil and place into an air fryer.

4. Cook until flaky, about 15 minutes.

5. Dip fish into reserved marinade during the last 5 minutes of cooking time.

Per serving: Calories: 237 Kcal; Fat: 10 g; Carbs: 15 g; Protein: 20 g; Sugar: 13 g; Sodium: 569 mg

73. Breaded Sea Scallops

Preparation time: 12 minutes

Cooking time: 8 minutes

Servings: 2

Ingredients:

- ½ cup finely crushed buttery crackers
- ½ teaspoon seafood seasoning
- 1 pound sea scallops, patted dry
- 1 serving cooking spray
- 2 tablespoons butter, melted
- ½ teaspoon garlic powder

Directions:

1. Preheat the air fryer to 390 °F.

2. Mix cracker crumbs, garlic powder, and seafood seasoning together in a shallow bowl. Place melted butter in another shallow bowl.

3. Dip each scallop into the melted butter and then roll in the breading until fully coated; set on a plate and repeat with remaining scallops.

4. Lightly spray the basket with cooking spray so that it doesn't stick to scallops.

5. Arrange scallops evenly in the basket so they're not touching each other.

6. Cook for 2 minutes. Turn scallops over gently with small spatula—they should be opaque after about 2 more minutes.

Per serving: Calories: 180 Kcal; Fat: 4 g; Carbs: 9 g; Protein: 28 g; Sugar: 1 g; Sodium: 230 mg

74. Honey Glazed Salmon

Preparation time: 2 minutes

Cooking time: 8 minutes

Servings: 4

Ingredients:

- 4 Salmon Fillets
- Black Pepper
- 1 tablespoon Honey
- Salt
- 2 teaspoons Soy Sauce
- 1 teaspoon Sesame Seeds

Directions:

1. Preheat your air fryer to 375°F (190°C). Sprinkle salt and black pepper on salmon fillet. Brush soy sauce into it.

2. Place the fillets in the basket, skin side down, and cook them for 8 minutes or until ready. Glaze each fish with honey, then sprinkle with sesame seeds just before serving.

3. Serve with a side of your choice.

Per serving: Calories: 262Kcal; Fat: 11g; Carbs: 5g; Protein: 34g; Sugar: 4g; Sodium: 158mg

75. Shrimp (Honey Lime)

Preparation time: 5 minutes

Cooking time: 5 minutes

Servings: 4

Ingredients:

- 1 lb large shrimp
- 1 ½ tablespoons lime juice
- 2 cloves garlic
- ⅛ teaspoon salt
- 1 ½ tablespoons honey
- 1 ½ tablespoons olive oil
- cilantro
- lime wedges

Directions:

1. In a large bowl, stir together the olive oil, lime juice, honey, garlic, and salt.

2. Marinate shrimps in this marinade for 20-30 minutes.

3. Heat the air fryer to 390°F/200°C.

4. Shake excess marinade off the shrimp and put them in the basket.

5. Cook for two minutes or until pink and cooked through.

Per serving: Calories: 187Kcal; Fat: 7g; Carbs: 7g; Protein: 23g; Sugar: 7g; Sodium: 955mg

76. Halibut

Preparation time: 10 minutes

Cooking time: 10 minutes

Servings: 2

Ingredients:

- 2 halibut filets
- 2 tablespoons melted butter
- 1/2 cup panko breadcrumbs
- 1 teaspoon herb and garlic seasoning

Directions:

1. Preheat the air fryer to 380 °F.

2. Pat each filet dry with paper towel, then mix the remaining ingredients and place in air fryer basket.

3. Cook at 380 °F for 8-10 minutes.

Per serving: Calories: 321Kcal; Fat: 15g; Carbs: 13g; Protein: 34g; Sugar: 1g; Sodium: 326mg

77. Tuna Cakes

Preparation time: 10 minutes

Cooking time: 12 minutes

Servings: 12

Ingredients:

- 2 - 12 oz. cans of chunk tuna in water
- 1/2 cup seasoned breadcrumbs
- 2 Tablespoon lemon juice
- 1/2 Teaspoon salt
- 2 eggs
- 4 Tablespoon mayo
- 1/2 diced white onion
- 1/2 Teaspoon black pepper

Directions:

1. Mix the ingredients in a large bowl.

2. Form the mixture into patties and place them into a cooking basket in your air fryer.

3. Cook at 375 °F for 12 minutes, flipping at half-time.

4. Remove and serve immediately.

Per serving: Calories: 83Kcal; Fat: 0g; Carbs: 4g; Protein: 5g; Sugar: 1g; Sodium: 260mg

78. Shrimp Tacos

Preparation time: 5 minutes

Cooking time: 8 minutes

Servings: 4

Ingredients:

- 1 Lb Peeled, Deveined Shrimp
- 1/2 teaspoon Chili Powder
- 1/4 teaspoon Cumin
- Pinch Salt
- 4 Flour Tortillas
- Sliced Avocado
- Cilantro
- Lime
- Crumbled Cotija Cheese
- Green Shredded Cabbage
- Pinch Pepper
- 1/4 teaspoon Onion Powder
- 1/2 teaspoon Garlic Powder
- 2 Tablespoons Oil

Directions:

1. In a bowl, toss shrimp with oil, chili powder, garlic powder, cumin, onion powder, salt, and pepper. Transfer to a greased air fryer basket.

2. Air fry at 400°F for 5-6 minutes.

3. Assemble tacos with shrimp and cabbage in tortillas; place them in the air fryer basket and air fry at 400°F for 1 minute to warm up the tortillas

4. Remove tacos from the basket and add toppings. Serve immediately.

Per serving: Calories: 454Kcal; Fat: 20g; Carbs 37g; Protein: 32g; Sugar: 1g; Sodium: 1375mg

79. Coconut Shrimp

Preparation time: 10 minutes

Cooking time: 12 minutes

Servings: 4

Ingredients:

- 1 pound shrimp *raw*
- ½ teaspoon salt
- 2 large eggs
- ¼ cup breadcrumbs
- Sweet chili sauce *for serving*
- ¼ cup all-purpose flour
- ¼ teaspoon black pepper
- ¾ cup unsweetened shredded coconut
- Cooking spray

Directions:

1. To make coconut shrimp, preheat the air fryer to 360°F.

2. Spray the basket with cooking spray.

3. To make the batter, whisk together flour, salt and pepper in one shallow bowl. Whisk together eggs and shredded coconut in another shallow bowl.

4. Combine panko breadcrumbs with salt-and-pepper seasoning in a third shallow bowl.

5. Dip shrimp into flour mixture, shaking off excess; then dredge into eggs; finally, press into coconut mixture to coat evenly.

6. Place on top of shrimp so they are not touching; spray top with oil or cooking spray.

7. Cook for 10-12 minutes, flipping halfway through until golden brown on both sides

Per serving: Calories: 304Kcal; Fat: 15g; Carbs: 13g; Protein: 28g; Sugar: 2g; Sodium: 1237mg

80. Fish Fillet

Preparation time: 5 minutes

Cooking time: 15 minutes

Servings: 8

Ingredients:

- 8 fish fillets
- 1 cup dry bread crumbs
- ¼ teaspoon chili powder
- ¼ teaspoon garlic powder or granules
- ½ teaspoon salt
- 1 tablespoon olive oil
- ½ teaspoon paprika
- ¼ teaspoon ground black pepper
- ¼ teaspoon onion powder

Directions:

1. When using frozen fish fillets, it is best to defrost them first.

2. Drizzle the fish with olive oil, and make sure that it is well coated with oil.

3. Prepare the bread crumbs by combining them with paprika, chili powder, black pepper, garlic powder, onion powder, and salt.

4. Cook the fish fillets in the air fryer for 12-15 minutes at 390°F (200°C).

5. After 8-10 minutes, open the air fryer and flip the fish fillets over onto their other side. Then continue cooking.

Per serving: Calories: 153Kcal; Fat: 3g; Carbs: 11g; Protein: 21g; Sugar: 0g; Sodium: 369mg

81. Honey Mustard Salmon

Preparation time: 5 minutes

Cooking time: 10 minutes

Servings: 2

Ingredients:

- 2 salmon fillets
- 2 tablespoons whole grain Dijon mustard
- 1/4 teaspoon smoked paprika
- Salt and pepper
- 2 tablespoons honey
- 1/2 teaspoon garlic powder
- 1 teaspoon lemon juice

Directions:

1. To make this recipe, combine the sauce ingredients.

2. Marinate the salmon in two-thirds (2/3) of the sauce for 30 minutes or toss the salmon fillets in the sauce until fully covered.

3. Preheat air fryer to 400°F and place the salmon fillets in the air fryer.

4. Baste the remaining marinade onto the salmon fillets. Air fry for 7-8 minutes, depending on your preference for browning.

Per serving: Calories: 268Kcal; Fat: 6.7g; Carbs: 18g; Protein: 31.8g; Sugar: 17g; Sodium: 502mg

82. Miso-Glazed Salmon

Preparation time: 20 minutes

Cooking time: 10 minutes

Servings: 2

Ingredients:

- 2 pieces of Salmon with the skin
- 1.5 Tablespoon of Soy Sauce
- 1.5 Tablespoon of Sake
- .5 Tablespoon of Sesame Oil
- 1 Tablespoon of Sugar

- 2.5 Tablespoon of Miso Paste

Directions:

1. Mix miso paste, soy sauce, sugar, sake, and sesame oil in a bowl.

2. Add salmon and rub well. Marinate for 20-40 minutes.

3. Spray the air fryer with oil and add salmon skin side down at 400 °F for 8 minutes.

4. Garnish with sesame seeds and green onion. ENJOY!

Per serving: Calories: 277Kcal; Fat: 10g; Carbs: 21g; Protein: 27g; Sugar: 16g; Sodium: 876mg

83. Tuna Melt

Preparation time: 7 minutes

Cooking time: 8 minutes

Servings: 1

Ingredients:

- 2 slices sandwich bread
- Temperature butter
- 1/2 cup tuna salad
- 1–2 tablespoons mayonnaise
- 1 1/2–2 slices cheddar cheese

Directions:

1. First, cover one side of bread with the mayo or room temp butter. Place that piece of bread into the air fryer basket, mayo-side down.

2. Next, put cheese slices on top of the bread. Use a spoon to push out the tuna salad so that it goes around each slice of cheese.

3. Finally, add one more piece of bread and coat one side in mayonnaise just like the other side.

4. Shut off the air fryer and set it to cook at 380°F for 8 minutes; then flip it over halfway through cooking time so that both sides are golden brown with melted cheese.

5. Remove from the basket and cut in half on a cutting board while still warm!

Per serving: Calories: 637Kcal; Fat: 34g; Carbs: 43g; Protein: 33g; Sugar: 1g; Sodium: mg

84. Air-Fryer Cajun Shrimp

Preparation time: 10 minutes

Cooking time: 20 minutes

Servings: 4

Ingredients:

- 1 tablespoon Cajun
- 24 cleaned and peeled extra jumbo shrimp
- 1 medium zucchini, 8 ounces
- 1 large red bell pepper,
- 2 tablespoons olive oil
- 6 ounces fully cooked Turkey
- 1 medium yellow squash
- 1/4 teaspoon kosher salt

Directions:

1. Take a bowl, combine the Cajun seasoning and shrimp. Toss to coat. Add the sausage, zucchini, squash, bell peppers, and salt.

2. Then add the oil to your air fryer basket and heat it up to 400°F. In batches (for smaller baskets), transfer the shrimp and vegetables to the air fryer basket and cook 8 minutes. Set aside.

3. Repeat with remaining shrimp and veggies. Once both batches are cooked, return them to the air fryer for 1 minute

Per serving: Calories: 284Kcal; Fat: 14g; Carbs: 8g; Protein: 31g; Sugar: 3g; Sodium: 1500mg

85. Salmon Patties

Preparation time: 15 minutes

Cooking time: 8 minutes

Servings: 4

Ingredients:

- 12 oz canned salmon
- ¼ cup mayo
- ½ cup breadcrumbs
- ½ teaspoon dried dill
- 2 eggs
- ¼ teaspoon salt
- lemon zested

Directions:

1. Mix the salmon (drained, mashed, and skin/bones removed if you'd like), eggs, mayo, salt, breadcrumbs, and dill in a large bowl.

2. Using a ½ cup measuring cup, firmly pack the mixture into the cup and tap it into your hand.

3. Pat gently to form patties that are no more than 1 inch thick and are of equal thickness across each patty.

4. Heat air fryer to 390°F. Spray basket with oil, then add patties into the basket.

5. Cook for 8 minutes cooldown period (1-2 minutes before cooked through).

Per serving: Calories: 298Kcal; Fat: 18g; Carbs: 10g; Protein: 24g; Sugar: 1g; Sodium: 689mg

86. Fish and Chips

Preparation time: 5 minutes

Cooking time: 10 minutes

Servings: 3

Ingredients:

- 16 ounces frozen French fries
- 1 cup panko bread crumbs
- 1/2 cup all-purpose flour
- 1/2 teaspoon garlic powder
- 1/4 teaspoon pepper
- 1/2 teaspoon salt
- 2 teaspoons paprika
- 1 egg
- 1 pounds fish fillets

Directions:

1. First, make the French fries. Freeze them first, then heat them in an air fryer at 400 °F for 15 minutes. Shake them a few times while they cook.

2. While the fries cook, preheat the oven to 250 °F and prepare three bowls: one for bread crumbs, another for egg, and a third for flour.

3. Cut the fish fillet into serving-size pieces (or stick-cut it if you prefer). Pat dry with paper towels and dip it into the flour mixture before frying it in oil or butter.

4. To make breaded air-fried potatoes, you'll need: flour, egg, and breadcrumbs. First, coat the potato pieces in flour.

5. Then dip them in an egg wash and coat with breadcrumbs; set aside until the next step. In order to keep it from sticking to your fingers while you work with it, use a vegetable oil spray instead of your hand.

6. Place the coated pieces on a baking sheet lined with aluminum foil or parchment paper; put them in the air-fryer at 400 °F for 10 minutes; then flip them over and cook until they're soft enough to easily flake with a fork or until they reach 145 °F on an indoor stovetop thermometer (if using an oven thermometer, cook for 10-12 minutes).

7. Serve with French fries and lemon slices over ice; top with tartar sauce if desired.

Per serving: Calories: 266Kcal; Fat: 6g; Carbs: 27g; Protein: 25g; Sugar: 2g; Sodium: 878mg

87. Scallops with Garlic Herb Butter

Preparation time: 5 minutes

Cooking time: 10 minutes

Servings: 3

Ingredients:

- 1 lb scallops dry scallops
- 1 Tablespoon minced garlic
- 1 teaspoon chopped parsley
- 1 teaspoon lemon juice
- 1 teaspoon kosher salt
- 2 Tablespoon unsalted butter melted

Directions:

1. Pat dry the scallops and set them aside. Preheat the air fryer to 400 °F.

2. Combine melted butter, garlic, salt, parsley, and lemon juice in a bowl; use some mixture on the bottom of the basket.

3. Place scallops in basket (no overlapping); spread remaining mixture on top of scallops.

4. Cook 8-10 minutes or until desired doneness.

Per serving: Calories: 176Kcal; Fat: 8g; Carbs: 6g; Protein: 18g; Sugar: 1g; Sodium: 1396mg

88. Miso Glazed Chilean Sea Bass

Preparation time: 5 minutes

Cooking time: 20 minutes

Servings: 2

Ingredients:

- 2 6 ounce chilean sea bass fillets
- 1/4 cup white miso paste
- 4 tablespoons maple syrup
- 1/2 teaspoon ginger paste
- Fresh black pepper
- olive oil for cooking
- 2 tablespoons mirin
- 1 tablespoon rice wine vinegar
- 1 tablespoon unsalted butter

Directions:

1. Heat the air fryer to 375° F. Brush olive oil on each fillet of fish, then finish with fresh cracked pepper.

2. Spritz the air fryer pan with olive oil and place the fish skin side down.

3. Cook for 12-15 minutes until the top turns golden brown and the internal temperature reaches 135° F.

4. While the fish is cooking, melt butter in a small saucepan over medium heat. When it's melted, add miso paste, rice wine vinegar, maple syrup, maple syrup, mirin and ginger paste; stir until combined before boiling over high heat for about 30 seconds.

5. Remove from heat immediately after boiling and set aside for 20 minutes to cool slightly before

serving with sliced green onions and/or sesame seeds.

Per serving: Calories: 524Kcal; Fat: 29g; Carbs 23g; Protein: 24g; Sugar: 15g; Sodium: 624mg

89. Air-Fryer Shrimps

Preparation time: 2 minutes

Cooking time: 8 minutes

Servings: 4

Ingredients:

- 1 pound large or jump shrimp
- 1/2 cup olive oil
- 3 garlic cloves minced
- 1 Tablespoon lemon juice
- 1 teaspoon Dijon mustard
- 1 Tablespoon Worcestershire sauce
- 2 Tablespoons soy sauce
- 1 Tablespoon Italian seasoning
- 1/4 cup red wine vinegar
- salt and pepper

Directions:

1. In a bowl, combine olive oil, red wine vinegar garlic, Italian seasoning, lemon juice, soy sauce Dijon Mustard, and Worcestershire sauce.

2. Add the shrimp and sprinkle salt and pepper then let it marinate for at least one hour o overnight. After marinating, remove the shrimp from the marinade and place them in the air fryer basket.

3. Cook at 400 °F for 8 minutes or until pink an cooked through.

Per serving: Calories: 372Kcal; Fat: 29g; Carbs: 3g Protein: 24g; Sugar: 1g; Sodium: 1442mg

90. Salmon with Maple Soy Glaze

Preparation time: 5 minutes

Cooking time: 8 minutes

Servings: 4

Ingredients:

- 3 Tablespoon pure maple syrup

- 1 Tablespoon sriracha hot sauce
- 4 wild salmon fillets, skinless
- 3 Tablespoon reduced sodium soy sauce
- 1 clove garlic

Directions:

1. Combine maple syrup, soy sauce, sriracha, and garlic in a small bowl.

2. Pour into a gallon-sized re-sealable bag and add the salmon.

3. Marinate for 20 to 30 minutes, turning once or twice. Lightly spray the basket with oil. Remove fish from marinade and pat dry with paper towels.

4. Place fish in an air fryer basket at 400°F for 7-8 minutes or longer, depending on the thickness of salmon.

5. Meanwhile, bring marinade to a simmer over medium-low heat; reduce until thickened into glaze; spoon over fish just before eating

Per serving: Calories: 292Kcal; Fat: 11g; Carbs: 12g; Protein: 35g; Sugar: 10g; Sodium: 797mg

91. Fish Tacos

Preparation time: 20 minutes

Cooking time: 12 minutes

Servings: 4

Ingredients:

- 24 oz firm white fish fillets
- 1 large avocado
- 1/4 cup red onion
- 1 Teaspoon salt divided
- 1/4 cup chipotle sauce
- corn tortillas
- 1 Tablespoon fresh lime juice
- 1/4 cup mayonnaise
- 2 Tablespoons fresh cilantro
- 2 medium oranges peeled and chopped
- 1 Tablespoons grill seasoning

Directions:

1. In a mixing bowl, stir together the avocado, orange, onion, cilantro, and half teaspoon of salt. Set aside.

2. In a separate mixing bowl, stir mayonnaise, chipotle sauce, and lime juice. Stir in half teaspoon of salt. Evenly sprinkle fish with grill seasoning.

3. Brush air fryer basket lightly with vegetable oil to prevent sticking. Arrange fish in single layer in basket.

4. Cook at 400 °F for 8 - 12 minutes or until internal temperature reaches 145 °F as measured by an instant-read thermometer. It is not necessary to flip fish during cooking.

5. Serve the fish tacos with warmed corn tortillas, avocado citrus salsa, and chipotle mayonnaise for a delicious meal.

Per serving: Calories: 230Kcal; Fat: 12g; Carbs: 18g; Protein: 22g; Sugar: 2g; Sodium: 326mg

92. Lobster Tails

Preparation time: 10 minutes

Cooking time: 10 minutes

Servings: 4

Ingredients:

- 4 lobster tails 4 oz each
- 1 tablespoon lemon zest
- salt and pepper to taste
- 1 tablespoon fresh parsley chopped
- 8 tablespoon butter unsalted
- 2 cloves garlic minced
- ½ teaspoon smoked paprika

Directions:

1. Cut the top shell off a lobster tail, then cut it in half. Spread the halves apart and put them in the air fryer basket with the meat facing up.

2. Preheat the Air fryer to 380 °F.

3. Add the butter and lemon zest to a small saucepan over medium heat. Add the garlic, salt,

pepper, and smoked paprika and cook for another minute.

4. Transfer this mixture to a smaller bowl and brush over the lobster tails.

5. Cook the lobster tails for 5 to 7 minutes or until the lobster meat is opaque. Serve with lemon wedges, sprinkled with parsley.

Per serving: Calories: 253Kcal; Fat: 23g; Carbs: 1g; Protein: 11g; Sugar: 1g; Sodium: 272mg

93. Shrimp Fajita

Preparation time: 10 minutes

Cooking time: 22 minutes

Servings: 12

Ingredients:

- 1 Red Bell Pepper
- 1/2 Cup Sweet Onion
- 1 Pound Medium Shrimp Tail-Off
- White Corn Tortillas
- Olive Oil Spray
- 2 Tablespoon of Fajita Seasoning
- 1 Green Bell Pepper

Directions:

1. To make this recipe, spray the air fryer basket with olive oil spray or line with foil. If you are using frozen shrimp, run cold water over it to get the ice off.

2. Add peppers and onion plus seasoning, then add a coat of olive oil spray. Mix it all together and cook at 390 °F for 12 minutes.

3. Open the lid and add in shrimp for the final 10 minutes of cook time before closing again.

4. Serve on warm tortillas with sauce on side.

Per serving: Calories: 86Kcal; Fat: 2g; Carbs: 6g; Protein: 10g; Sugar: 1g; Sodium: 420mg

94. Fish Nuggets

Preparation time: 10 minutes

Cooking time: 10 minutes

Servings: 2

Ingredients:

- 2 3oz filets of thick white fish
- 1/2 cup almond flour
- 1/2 Teaspoon pepper
- 1/2 Teaspoon smoked paprika
- Spray oil
- 1/2 tsp garlic powder
- 1 Teaspoon salt
- 1 egg

Directions:

1. Cut the fillets into bite-size pieces and whisk the egg in a small shallow bowl.

2. Mix the almond flour, salt, pepper, garlic powder, and smoked paprika together in a separate shallow bowl.

3. Dip each fish nugget in the egg to coat it thoroughly before dipping it in the almond flour mixture. Place each breaded nugget on an air fryer tray and spray lightly with cooking oil—I used spray avocado oil.

4. Cook at 425°F for 10 minutes until golden brown on all sides.

5. Remove from heat and allow to cool slightly before serving!

Per serving: Calories: 263Kcal; Fat: 7.6g; Carbs: 6.4g; Protein: 22g; Sugar: 1.2g; Sodium: 1291mg

95. Halibut Pistachio Crusted

Preparation time: 10 minutes

Cooking time: 8 minutes

Servings:

Ingredients:

- ¼ cup crumbled goat cheese
- 2 Tablespoons panko breadcrumbs
- ½ teaspoon lemon zest
- 1 teaspoon olive oil
- salt to taste
- Lemon wedges.
- 1/8 teaspoon garlic powder

- 2 halibut fillets
- 1 green onion, minced
- 2 Tablespoons finely chopped pistachio

Directions:

1. Set the temperature of the air fryer to 380°F for 3 minutes.

2. Stir goat cheese, chopped pistachios, panko breadcrumbs, and scallion in a small bowl; set aside.

3. Pat dry halibut fillets with paper towel; brush top with olive oil.

4. Coat with pistachio mixture; press to help adhere. Air fry for 6 to 10 minutes or until fish flakes easily with fork.

5. Serve with lemon wedges and side dish of choice (such as mashed potatoes). Enjoy!

Per serving: Calories: 159Kcal; Fat: 10g; Carbs: 11g; Protein: 8g; Sugar: 2g; Sodium: 198mg

Air-Fryer Tilapia

Preparation time: 10 minutes

Cooking time: 7 minutes

Servings: 2

Ingredients:

- 2 fresh tilapia filets
- 1/2 Teaspoon salt
- 1 Teaspoon garlic powder
- 1/4 Teaspoon chili powder
- 1 Teaspoon dried parsley
- 1 Teaspoon paprika
- 1/4 Teaspoon black pepper
- 1/2 Teaspoon olive oil

Mango Salsa

- 1 ripe mango, peeled and cubed
- 1/4 tsp salt
- juice from 1/2 lime
- 1/4 cup chopped cilantro
- 2 tablespoons diced red onion

Directions:

1. Mix the salt, pepper, spices, and parsley in a mixing bowl or plate.

2. Rub each tilapia filet with olive oil, then dredge in seasoning mixture to coat each filet on both sides.

3. Preheat the air fryer for 3 minutes at 370 °F.

4. Place seasoned tilapia filets in air fryer basket and set to fish setting (or 330 °F), and cook for 7 minutes.

5. While the fish cooks, prepare mango salsa by mixing all ingredients together in bowl.

6. When fish is done, place on plate over bed of cooked rice or in taco shells (optional). Top with mango salsa!

Per serving: Calories: 303Kcal; Fat: 21g; Carbs: 1.3g; Protein: 27g; Sugar: 0g; Sodium: 251mg

96. Corn and Crab Cake

Preparation time: 15 minutes

Cooking time: 30 minutes

Servings: 8

Ingredients:

- 1 cup corn kernels,
- 1 cup about 30 reduced-fat Ritz crackers, crushed
- 1 whole egg plus 2 egg whites
- 1/4 cup minced red bell pepper
- 2 Tablespoon fat free yogurt
- 1 lemon, juiced
- salt and pepper to taste
- cooking spray
- 16 oz premium lump crab meat
- 1/4 cup fresh parsley
- 2 Tablespoon light mayonnaise
- 4 scallions, chopped fine

Directions:

1. In a large bowl, combine corn, crushed crackers, eggs, scallions, pepper, and mayo.

2. Mix well. Fold in crab meat and gently shape into 8 patties using a 1/2 cup measuring cup.

3. Air fry in batches at 370°F until the edges are golden, about 10 to 12 minutes.

4. Turn halfway through cooking.

Per serving: Calories: 97Kcal; Fat: 3g; Carbs: 7.5g; Protein: 11g; Sugar: 1.5g; Sodium: 385mg

97. Cod Fillet

Preparation time: 10 minutes

Cooking time: 15 minutes

Servings: 4

Ingredients:

- 1 pound cod filets
- 1/2 cup flour
- 1/2 teaspoon salt
- 1/2 cup grated parmesan
- 1/2 teaspoon garlic powder
- olive oil spray if needed
- 2 teaspoons old bay seasoning
- 1 cup Panko
- 2 large eggs
- salt and pepper

Directions:

1. Season the cod filets with salt and pepper.

2. In a large bowl, combine flour, eggs, and Panko breadcrumbs; season with garlic powder, parmesan cheese, and old bay seasoning.

3. Dip each filet into the egg mixture, then coat with Panko crumbs.

4. Place in an air fryer basket; cook at 400°F for 10 minutes.

5. Turn over; cook another 3-5 minutes or until an internal temperature of 145°F has been reached.

Per serving: Calories: 303Kcal; Fat: 8g; Carbs: 24g; Protein: 32g; Sugar: 1g; Sodium: 689mg

98. Tuna Steak

Preparation time: 5 minutes

Cooking time: 2 minutes

Servings: 2

Ingredients:

- 2 tuna steaks
- 1 teaspoon olive oil
- Salt
- pepper

DIPPING SAUCE

- 2 Green onions
- 2 Tablespoon coconut amino
- 1 Tablespoon lime juice
- 1 Tablespoon of water
- 1/2 teaspoon minced garlic

Directions:

1. Set the temperature of the air fryer at 370°F fc 5 minutes.

2. Coat all sides of the ahi tuna steaks with oliv oil and season with salt and pepper.

3. Add the steaks to the air fryer basket, then a fry at 370°F for 2 minutes on each side or unt desired doneness.

4. Meanwhile, take a bowl and mix coconu amino, green onion, lime juice, water, and garl into a small bowl; set aside.

5. Remove steaks from basket and thinly slice serve with lime dipping sauce on the side.

Per serving: Calories: 132Kcal; Fat: 3g; Carbs: 5g Protein: 21g; Sugar: 3g; Sodium: 457mg

99. Bacon Wrapped Scallops

Preparation time: 10 minutes

Cooking time: 14 minutes

Servings: 8

Ingredients:

- 8 slices bacon
- 1 teaspoon olive oil

- salt & pepper
- 8 large sea scallops
- ½ teaspoon old bay seasoning
- 2 tablespoons maple syrup

Directions:

1. Preheat your air fryer to 350°F. Fry 3-4 strips of bacon in the air fryer for 3-4 minutes or until just slightly cooked and some of the fat has rendered out.

2. Remove bacon from the air fryer.

3. Wrap one section of bacon around each scallop. Secure with a toothpick or thread onto short skewers.

4. Brush each scallop with maple syrup before placing it in an air fryer at 350°F for 11-13 minutes.

5. Cook until bacon is crisp, but not for too long.

Per serving: Calories: 120Kcal; Fat: 3g; Carbs: 4g; Protein: 5g; Sugar: 3g; Sodium: 205mg

CHAPTER 5: Meat Recipes

100. Chicken Cordon Bleu

Preparation time: 20 minutes

Cooking time: 10 minutes

Servings: 2

Ingredients:

- 1/8 teaspoon salt
- 2 boneless skinless chicken breast halves
- Cooking spray
- 1/2 cup panko bread crumbs
- 1/8 teaspoon pepper
- 2 slices deli ham
- 1 slice aged Swiss cheese, halved

Sauce:

- Dash pepper
- 1/8 teaspoon salt
- 1/2 tablespoon all-purpose flour
- 2 tablespoons finely shredded Swiss cheese
- 1/4 cup 2% milk
- 1/8 cup dry white wine

Directions:

1. First, preheat the air fryer to 365 °F. Sprinkle chicken breasts with salt and pepper. Place on a greased tray in the air fryer basket and cook for 10 minutes.

2. Top each chicken breast with a slice of ham, folding it in half and covering as much of the breast as possible. Sprinkle bread crumbs over each piece.

3. Carefully spritz them with cooking spray. Cook until the internal temperature reaches 165 °F —if not, cook for 5-7 more minutes.

4. For sauce: Mix flour and milk in a small saucepan until smooth and well combined. Bring to a boil, Stir it until it thickens.

5. Reduce heat to medium; stir in wine; cook 2-3 minutes more or until cheese is melted and sauce is thickened and bubbly.

6. Sprinkle salt and Black pepper; keep warm over low heat until ready to serve.

Per serving: Calories: 272 Kcal; Fat: 8 g; Carbs: 14 g; Protein: 32 g; Sugar: 2 g; Sodium: 519 mg

101. Turkey Croquettes

Preparation time: 20 minutes

Cooking time: 10 minutes

Servings: 4

Ingredients:

- 1/4 cup grated Parmesan cheese
- 1/4 cup shredded Swiss cheese
- Butter-flavored cooking spray
- 1/2 shallot, finely chopped
- 1 teaspoon1 minced fresh rosemary
- 1 cup mashed potatoes
- Sour cream
- 1/2 teaspoon minced fresh sage
- 1/4 teaspoon salt
- 1/8 teaspoon pepper
- 1/4 cups panko bread crumbs
- 2 cups finely chopped cooked turkey
- 1 large egg
- 1 tablespoon water

Directions:

1. Preheat the air fryer to 350°F. Put together a large bowl that contains mashed potatoes, cheeses, shallot, rosemary, sage, salt, and pepper. Mix these ingredients together thoroughly but lightly. Shape twelve 1-inch-thick patties out of the mixture.

2. Take a mixing bowl, whisk together the egg and add some water. Place bread crumbs in another

shallow bowl, and dip croquettes into the egg mixture, then into bread crumbs to coat.

3. Working in batches, place half the croquettes in a single layer on a greased tray. Spritz with cooking spray. Cook until golden brown, 4-5 minutes. Turn over; spritz with cooking spray again. Cook until golden brown, 4-5 minutes longer. Garnish with sour cream if desired.

Per serving: Calories: 321 Kcal; Fat: 12.1 g; Carbs: 22 g; Protein: 29 g; Sugar: 2 g; Sodium: 673 mg

102. Pork Chops

Preparation time: 10 minutes

Cooking time: 15 minutes

Servings: 2

Ingredients:

- 1/4 cup almond flour
- 1/8 cup grated Parmesan cheese
- 1/2 teaspoon paprika
- 1/2 teaspoon garlic powder
- Cooking spray
- 1/2 teaspoon Creole seasoning
- 2 boneless pork loin chops

Directions:

1. Preheat the air fryer to 375°F. Take a large bowl; mix almond flour, cheese, garlic powder, Creole seasoning, and paprika. Coat pork chops with the mixture; shake off any excess flour mixture. Working in batches as needed, place chops in single layer on greased tray in the air-fryer basket; spritz with cooking spray.

2. Cook until golden brown, 12-15 minutes or until a thermometer reads 145°, turning halfway through cooking and spritzing with additional cooking spray. Remove and keep warm. Repeat with remaining chops.

Per serving: Calories: 310 Kcal; Fat: 16 g; Carbs: 4 g; Protein: 36 g; Sugar: 0 g; Sodium: 308 mg

103. Steak Fajitas

Preparation time: 15 minutes

Cooking time: 15 minutes

Servings: 4

Ingredients:

- 1/4 cup diced red onion
- 4 whole wheat tortillas, warmed
- 1/8 cup lime juice
- 1 teaspoon ground cumin, divided
- 1/2 jalapeno pepper, seeded and minced
- Sliced avocado and lime wedges
- 2 tablespoons minced fresh cilantro
- 1 large tomato, seeded and chopped
- 1/4 teaspoon salt, divided
- 1/2 beef flank steak
- 1/2 large onion, halved and sliced

Directions:

1. For salsa, mix first 5 ingredients (lemon juice, lime juice, onion, cumin, and salt) in a small bowl; let stand until serving. Meanwhile, sprinkle steak with the remaining cumin and salt; place on greased tray in air-fryer basket.

2. Cook until the internal temperature of the meat reaches desired doneness (for medium-rare, the reading should be 135°F; medium 140°F, medium-well 145°F), 6-8 minutes per side.

3. Remove from basket and let stand 5 minutes before slicing thinly across the grain. Serve with onion and salsa.

Per serving: Calories: 309 Kcal; Fat: 9 g; Carbs: 29 g; Protein: 27 g; Sugar: 3 g; Sodium: 498 mg

104. Coconut-Crusted Turkey Fingers

Preparation time: 20 minutes

Cooking time: 10 minutes

Servings: 4

Ingredients:

- 1/2 pounds turkey breast tenderloins, cut into
- 1 tablespoon sesame seeds, toasted

- 1 teaspoon sesame oil
- 1/4 teaspoon salt
- 1/4 cup sweetened coconut, lightly toasted (shredded)
- 1/4 cup dry bread crumbs
- 1/2-inch strips 1 large egg white
- Cooking spray

Dipping sauce:

- 2/3 cup unsweetened pineapple juice
- Grated lime zest and lime wedges
- 1/4 cup plum sauce
- 1/2 teaspoons prepared mustard
- 1/2 teaspoon cornstarch

Directions:

1. To prepare the turkey, preheat the air fryer to 400°F. Whisk 2 egg whites and 2 tablespoons of oil in a shallow bowl.

2. In another shallow bowl, mix 4 teaspoons of coconut flour, 1 tablespoon of bread crumbs (preferably egg-free), 1 teaspoon of sesame seeds, and 1/4 teaspoon of salt.

3. Dip the turkey in this mixture, then into another mixture of 4 egg yolks, 1/2 cup water, and 2 tablespoons of oil. Pat this mixture onto the turkey so that it sticks well.

4. Finally, place your turkey in a single layer on greased trays in your air fryer basket.

5. Cook until golden brown – about 3-4 minutes – turning once or twice during cooking so that both sides get cooked evenly. Serve with grated lime zest for garnish if desired.

Per serving: Calories: 292 Kcal; Fat: 9 g; Carbs: 24 g; Protein: 31 g; Sugar: 5 g; Sodium: 517 mg

105. Buttermilk Fried Chicken

Preparation time: 10 minutes

Cooking time: 15 minutes

Servings: 2

Ingredients:

- ½ cup low-fat buttermilk
- 1/8 teaspoon hot sauce
- ½ pound boneless, skinless chicken breasts
- Cooking spray
- 1/8 teaspoon salt
- 1/8 teaspoon coarse-ground black pepper
- 4 tablespoons corn flakes
- 2 tablespoons stone-ground cornmeal
- ½ teaspoon garlic powder
- 1 teaspoon paprika

Directions:

1. Take a small mixing bowl, mix the buttermilk and hot sauce together. Place the chicken in the buttermilk mixture. Allow to stand for 15 minutes

2. Place cornflakes into the work bowl of food processor. Process until coarse crumbs form. Add cornmeal, garlic powder, paprika, salt and pepper and pulse until evenly mixed. Pour crumbs into shallow bowl.

3. Coat chicken evenly in cornflake mixture; place pieces on wire rack.

4. Place the chicken in the air fryer basket and spray with nonstick cooking spray.

5. Cook for 7 minutes at 375°F, turning occasionally. Cook for an additional 7–10 minutes or until done and a meat thermometer inserted into the center registers 165°F.

Per serving: Calories: 160 Kcal; Fat: 3.5 g; Carbs: 1 g; Protein: 24 g; Sugar: 0 g; Sodium: 190 mg

106. Air-Fryer Meatloaf

Preparation time: 10 minutes

Cooking time: 35 minutes

Servings: 4

Ingredients:

- 2 pounds ground beef
- 1/4 cup milk
- 1 packet McCormick's meatloaf seasoning
- 2 eggs

- 2/3 cup breadcrumbs
- 1 tablespoon Worcestershire sauce

For Topping

- 1/2 tablespoon Worcestershire sauce
- 1/2 cup light brown sugar
- 1 tablespoon Dijon mustard
- 1 cup ketchup

Directions:

1. Prepare the meatloaf by combining the beef, eggs, milk, bread crumbs, meatloaf seasoning, and Worcestershire sauce in a large bowl.

2. Form it into a loaf shape using your hands and place it in your air fryer for 25 minutes.

3. While the meatloaf is cooking combine the ketchup with brown sugar and Dijon mustard.

4. After 25 minutes spoon 1/4 cup of the topping mixture onto the meatloaf and place it back in the air fryer for 5 to 10 minutes more until it reaches 165°F.

5. Remove from heat and serve by topping it with additional ketchup mixture!

Per serving: Calories: 189Kcal; Fat: 9g; Carbs: 13g; Protein: 14g; Sugar: 2g; Sodium: 475mg

107. Pork Chops

Preparation time: 5 minutes

Cooking time: 16 minutes

Servings: 4

Ingredients:

- 4 boneless pork chops
- 1/4 teaspoon sugar
- 1/2 teaspoon granulated onion
- 1/2 teaspoon celery seed
- 1/2 teaspoon salt
- 1/2 teaspoon granulated garlic
- 1/2 teaspoon parsley
- 2 teaspoons oil

Directions:

1. Combine the seasonings, then sprinkle them on both sides of the pork chops.

2. After adding the oil and rubbing it in, cook the pork chops at 350°F for 5 minutes per side for thin chops and 8 minutes per side for thick ones.

3. When done, the center of each chop should reach about 145° F.

4. Go to 155-160° F for well-done pork chops.

Per serving: Calories: 229Kcal; Fat: 3g; Carbs: g; Protein: 29g; Sugar: 4g; Sodium: 355mg

108. Crispy Pork Belly

Preparation time: 10 minutes

Cooking time: 30 minutes

Servings: 4

Ingredients:

- 1 pound pork belly
- 1 teaspoon of Salt
- 1 teaspoon Black Pepper
- 6 cloves Garlic
- 2 Bay Leaves
- 2 tablespoons Soy Sauce

Directions:

1. Cut the pork belly into three pieces so that they cook more evenly.

2. Put all ingredients into the inner liner of an Instant Pot or pressure cooker.

3. Cook at high pressure for 15 minutes. Allow 10 minutes for natural release, then remove to a plate using tongs and allow to drain for 10 minutes.

4. Cut each chunk into 2 long slices, then place in air fryer basket and roast at 400°F for almost 15 minutes or until fatty bits are crispy.

5. Serve hot with rice and soy sauce.

Per serving: Calories: 594Kcal; Fat: 60g; Carbs: g; Protein: 11g; Sugar: g; Sodium: 36mg

109. Bacon Wrapped Hot-Dog

Preparation time: 5 minutes

Cooking time: 10 minutes

Servings: 8

Ingredients:

- 8 Hot Dogs
- 8 Bacon Strips

Directions:

1. Wrap each hot dog with the desired amount of bacon.

2. Place 4 hot dogs in an air fryer basket. Make sure to space out hot dogs so that air can circulate around them and they won't overlap as they cook.

3. Set your air fryer to 360°F and cook for 15 minutes.

4. Check your hot dogs for doneness, cook another 1-2 minutes if necessary until they are cooked to your liking.

Per serving: Calories: 203Kcal; Fat: 15g; Carbs: 9g; Protein: 8g; Sugar: g; Sodium: 453mg

110. Crusted Chicken

Preparation time: 5 minutes

Cooking time: 12 minutes

Servings: 4

Ingredients:

- 1 pound chicken tenders
- 1 teaspoon Black Pepper
- 1/4 cup Coarse-Ground Mustard
- 1 cup finely-crushed pecans
- 1 teaspoon Salt
- 1/2 teaspoon Smoked Paprika
- 2 tablespoons Sugar-Free Maple Syrup

Directions:

1. To make the pecan crusted chicken tender bites, place the chicken tenders in a large bowl and add salt, pepper, and smoked paprika.

2. Mix well until the chicken is coated with the spices. Pour in maple syrup and mustard and mix well. Place finely-crushed pecans on a plate.

3. Take one chicken tender and roll it into the crushed pecans until both sides are coated.

4. Brush off any excess using an offset spatula once you've finished rolling each tender around in the pecan crumbles; this will help them stay put as you continue to fry them in the basket of air fryer at 350°F.

5. Once all of your chicken tenders have been coated with crushed pecans and brushed off once more, place them into your air fryer basket and cook for 12 minutes until cooked through.

Per serving: Calories: 325Kcal; Fat: 21g; Carbs: 8g; Protein: 27g; Sugar: 3g; Sodium: mg

111. Turkish Chicken Kebab

Preparation time: 45 minutes

Cooking time: 15 minutes

Servings: 4

Ingredients:

- 1/4 cup Greek Yogurt
- 1 Tablespoon Minced Garlic
- 1 Tablespoon Tomato Paste
- 1 Tablespoon Oil
- 1 Tablespoon Lemon Juice
- 1 Teaspoon Salt
- 1 Teaspoon Ground Cumin
- 1 Teaspoon Smoked Paprika
- 1/2 Teaspoon Ground Cinnamon
- 1/2 Teaspoon Ground Black Pepper
- 1/2 Teaspoon Cayenne Pepper
- 1 lb Boneless Skinless Chicken Thighs

Directions:

1. Take a large mixing bowl, mix Greek yogurt, garlic, tomato paste, lemon juice, oil, salt, and spices until evenly blended.

2. Add chicken pieces and mix well until coated with marinade.

3. Allow chicken to marinate for 30 minutes or up to 24 hours in the refrigerator.

4. Remove the chicken from the refrigerator and place it in a single layer on an air fryer basket lined with paper towels.

5. Set the air fryer to 370°F and cook for 10 minutes.

6. Open air fryer and flip over chicken pieces; cook for another 5 minutes at 370°F until the internal temperature reaches 165° F before serving.

Per serving: Calories: 298Kcal; Fat: 23g; Carbs: 4g; Protein: 20g; Sugar: 1g; Sodium: mg

112. Air-Fryer Crispy Chicken Wings

Preparation time: 5 minutes

Cooking time: 20 minutes

Servings: 2

Ingredients:

- 12 chicken wings
- 1 Tablespoon chili powder
- 1/2 Tablespoon baking POWDER
- 1/2 tsp kosher salt
- 1 Teaspoon granulated garlic

Directions:

1. Dry the wings with paper towels. Add salt, chili powder, and baking powder; rub all over the wings. Let them sit for 15 minutes.

2. Lightly oil an air fryer cooking rack with cooking oil to prevent sticking or burning. Arrange the wings on the rack, so there is space between them for free air circulation.

3. Set the air fryer temperature to 410°F and cook for 20 minutes or until your chicken is fully cooked and you see a golden brown top.

4. If you like your wings extra crispy, add 5 more minutes to the cooking time above and check them again when they're done cooking.

Per serving: Calories: 659Kcal; Fat: 46g; Carbs: 4g; Protein: 53g; Sugar: 0g; Sodium: 861mg

113. Whole Chicken

Preparation time: 5 minutes

Cooking time: 60 minutes

Servings: 6

Ingredients:

- 1 5 pound Whole chicken
- 1 Tablespoon Kosher Salt
- 1 teaspoon Garlic powder
- ½ teaspoon Dried basil
- ½ teaspoon Dried thyme
- 2 Tablespoons avocado oil
- 1 teaspoon ground black pepper
- 1 teaspoon Paprika
- ½ teaspoon Dried oregano

Directions:

1. Combine all of the seasonings with a bit of oil to make a paste, then spread it over your chicken.

2. Spray the basket of air fryer with cooking spray, then place the chicken in it breast side down.

3. Cook at 360°F for 50 minutes or until the breast meat reaches an internal temperature of 165°F.

Per serving: Calories: 271Kcal; Fat: 6.4g; Carbs: 1g; Protein: 24.8g; Sugar: 0.3g; Sodium: 364mg

114. Roast Beef

Preparation time: 5 minutes

Cooking time: 35 minutes

Servings: 6

Ingredients:

- 2lb beef roast
- 1 medium onion
- 2 teaspoons rosemary and thyme
- 1 tablespoon olive oil
- 1 teaspoon salt

Directions:

1. Preheat the air fryer to 390°F (200°C). Wash the beef roast using paper towels and pat it dry. Mix sea salt, rosemary, and oil on a plate.

2. Place the roast in the mixture, cover, and refrigerate for at least 1 hour. Place the beef in this mixture and turn so that it gets an even coating. If using onion, cut it into halves and place it in the basket.

3. Set up your air fryer. Let it heat up for 5 minutes, and you're good to go!

4. When the cooking time is up, change the temperature to 360°F (180°C). Flip the beef roast over half way through cooking if required by your air fryer.

5. Set it to cook for an additional 30 minutes to achieve a medium-rare steak. It's best to monitor its temperature with a meat thermometer to ensure that it's cooked to your liking. Check it early and cook for additional 5 minute intervals if you prefer well done meat.

Per serving: Calories: 212Kcal; Fat: 7g; Carbs: 2g; Protein: 33g; Sugar: 1g; Sodium: 282mg

115. Beef Kababs

Preparation time: 30 minutes

Cooking time: 10 minutes

Servings: 4

Ingredients:

- 1 lb. beef chuck ribs cut in 1-inch pieces
- 2 Tablespoons soy sauce
- 1/2 onion
- 1/3 cup sour cream
- 1 bell peppers
- 8 6-inch skewers

Directions:

1. Mix sour cream and soy sauce in a medium bowl. Add beef chunks and marinate for at least 30 minutes, but preferably overnight.

2. Cut bell pepper and onion; soak wooden skewers in water for 10 minutes.

3. Use a thread to tie the beef, onions, and peppers onto wooden skewers to make kebabs; sprinkle with some freshly ground black pepper.

4. Cook in preheated to 400°F air fryer for 1 minutes, turning half way through cooking time.

Per serving: Calories: 250Kcal; Fat: 15g; Carbs: 4g Protein: 23g; Sugar: 2g; Sodium: 609mg

116. Ultimate Lamb Burgers

Preparation time: 3 minutes

Cooking time: 18 minutes

Servings: 4

Ingredients:

Lamb Burger

- 650 g Minced Lamb
- 1 Teaspoon Harissa Paste
- Salt & Pepper
- 2 Teaspoons Garlic Puree
- 1 Tablespoon Moroccan Spice

Greek Dip

- 3 Tablespoons Greek Yoghurt
- ½ Tsp Oregano
- 1 Tsp Moroccan Spice
- 1 Small Lemon juice only

Directions:

1. In a mixing bowl, combine the ingredients for your lamb burgers.

2. Use a burger press to shape them into patties and place them in an air fryer. Cook them at 180°C/360°F for 18 minutes.

3. While they are cooking, prepare your Greek Dip.

4. Mix together all of its ingredients until they're well combined, and serve it with your lamb burgers.

Per serving: Calories: 478Kcal; Fat: 38g; Carbs: 3g; Protein: 28g; Sugar: 1g; Sodium: 101mg

117. Rack of Lamb

Preparation time: 30 minutes

Cooking time: 22 minutes

Servings: 4

Ingredients:

- 1 rack of lamb
- 1 teaspoon black pepper
- 1/2 teaspoon salt
- 1/2 teaspoon dried thyme
- 1/2 teaspoon coriander seeds
- 1 cup panko
- 1 tablespoon marjoram
- 1 tablespoon olive oil
- 1 tablespoon coffee grounds
- 1/2 teaspoon dried rosemary leaves
- 1/2 teaspoon smoked paprika
- 1 head garlic
- 1/4 cup fresh parsley

Directions:

1. Preheat the air fryer to 400°F.

2. Cut a top off of an onion and place it onto a small sheet of foil. Drizzle with olive oil, sprinkle with sea salt, and then wrap.

3. Cook for 25 minutes. While the garlic is cooking, purée it in a food processor and add parsley, marjoram, ¼ cup panko breadcrumbs, black pepper, coffee grounds (use less if you want a milder flavor), truffle salt, rosemary (use less if you want a milder flavor), thyme (use less if you want a milder flavor), paprika (use less if you want a milder flavor) and coriander seeds (use less if you want a milder flavor).

4. Pulse in another 10 seconds after each ingredient is added until they are well combined into one uniform mixture.

5. Spread this mixture out onto a plate. Preheat your air fryer to 400 °F for 5 minutes before putting on your rack of lamb bone side down and cook it this way for 3 minutes per side.

Per serving: Calories: 570Kcal; Fat: 47g; Carbs: 15g; Protein: 21g; Sugar: 1g; Sodium: 474mg

118. Air-Fryer Spicy Lamb Sirloin Steak

Preparation time: 40 minutes

Cooking time: 15 minutes

Servings: 4

Ingredients:

- 1-pound boneless lamb sirloin steaks
- 1/2 - 1 teaspoon Cayenne Pepper
- 1 teaspoon Ground Cinnamon
- 1 teaspoon Garam Masala
- 4 slices Ginger
- 1/2 Onion
- 5 cloves Garlic
- 1 teaspoon ground fennel
- 1/2 teaspoon Ground Cardamom
- 1 teaspoon Kosher Salt

Directions:

1. In a blender, add all ingredients except the lamb chops.

2. Pulse for about 3-4 minutes until the onion is minced and all ingredients are blended.

3. Slice into the lamb chops so they can soak up some of the marinade. Add the blended spices mixture and rub well.

4. Allow mixture to rest for 30 minutes or up to 24 hours in the refrigerator before cooking.

5. Let the air fryer reach 330°F (for 15 minutes), place one steak in the basket, and flip halfway through cooking time.

6. Use a meat thermometer to ensure that the internal temperature reaches 150°F for medium-well cooked meat. Serve with rice or noodles as desired.

Per serving: Calories: 182Kcal; Fat: 7g; Carbs: 3g; Protein: 24g; Sugar: 0g; Sodium: 445mg

119. Rib-Eye Steak with Blue Cheese

Preparation time: 15 minutes

Cooking time: 7 minutes

Servings: 2

Ingredients:

- 32 ounce Rib Eye Steaks (two steaks)
- 1.5 teaspoon Ground Black Pepper
- 2 Tablespoons Blue Cheese Butter
- 2 teaspoons Kosher Salt
- 1 teaspoon Garlic Powder

Directions:

1. Preheat your air fryer to 400°F or the highest temperature possible.

2. Coat both sides of each steak with salt, garlic powder, and pepper. Then, press the seasonings into the meat using your hand until they are completely covered.

3. Open up the air fryer and quickly place both steaks into the basket; close it back up and cook at 400°F for 4 minutes.

4. After that time has passed, flip the steaks over on their other side to cook for an additional 3 minutes before turning off your machine and leaving them to rest for 1 minute before serving hot with blue cheese butter on top.

Per serving: Calories: 829Kcal; Fat: 60g; Carbs: 2g; Protein: 69g; Sugar: 0g; Sodium: 2602mg

120. Air-Fryer Meatballs

Preparation time: 30 minutes

Cooking time: 10 minutes

Servings: 4

Ingredients:

- 1 pound lean ground beef
- 2 tablespoons heavy whipping cream
- 1/2 cup shredded mozzarella cheese
- 1 garlic clove,
- 1 large egg
- 1/2 cup Parmesan cheese

Sauce

- 1/4 cup heavy whipping cream
- 1 can tomato sauce with basil, garlic and oregano
- 2 tablespoons pesto

Directions:

1. Preheat your air fryer to 350°F. In a large bowl, combine the first five ingredients. Add the beef; mix lightly but thoroughly.

2. Shape into 1-1/2-in. balls and place them in a single layer on greased trays in your air fryer basket. Cook until lightly browned and cooked through, 8-10 minutes.

3. Meanwhile, in a small saucepan, mix the sauce ingredients and heat over medium heat until warm; serve with meatballs.

Per serving: Calories: 404Kcal; Fat: 27g; Carbs: 7g; Protein: 31g; Sugar: 3g; Sodium: 799mg

121. Stuffed Meat Loaf Slices

Preparation time: 30 minutes

Cooking time: 15 minutes

Servings: 6

Ingredients:

- 2 cups mashed potatoes
- Butter (melted)
- 1/2 cup Miracle Whip
- 1/4 cup chopped celery
- 1/4 teaspoon salt
- 1/4 teaspoon pepper
- 1/4 teaspoon ground mustard
- 1 green onion, chopped
- 1/3 cup grated Parmesan cheese
- 2 hard-boiled large eggs

Meat loaf:

- 1-1/4 pounds ground beef
- 1/4 cup dry bread crumbs
- 1 teaspoon salt

- 1 large egg, lightly beaten

Sauce:

- 1 green onion, sliced
- 1/2 cup Miracle Whip
- 1/4 cup milk

Directions:

1. To make the beef filling, mix the following ingredients in a large bowl. In a separate bowl, beat together an egg and bread crumbs with salt. Add the beef to this mixture; mix lightly but thoroughly.

2. On a large piece of heavy-duty foil, pat the mixture into a 14x8-in. rectangle. Spread the filling over the top to within 1 in. of edges; then roll it up jelly-roll style, starting with one short side and removing any foil as you go along. Seal the seam and ends; then place on a large plate or platter lined with paper towels so that it can be handled easily later on while cooking.

3. Refrigerate overnight before cooking.

4. Preheat the air fryer to 325°F .

5. Cut the roll into 6 slices. Place the slices on a greased tray and cook them for 12-15 minutes, or until their internal temperature reaches 160°F.

6. Mix the sauce ingredients; serve with meat loaf.

Per serving: Calories: 439Kcal; Fat: 28g; Carbs: 20g; Protein: 24g; Sugar: 5g; Sodium: 1187mg

122. **Beef Wellington Wontons**

Preparation time: 35 minutes

Cooking time: 10 minutes

Servings: 3 Dozens

Ingredients:

- 1/2 pound lean ground beef
- 1 tablespoon olive oil
- 1-1/2 teaspoons chopped shallot
- 1/4 cup dry red wine
- 1/2 teaspoon salt
- 1 package wonton wrappers

- 1 tablespoon water
- Cooking spray
- 1 large egg
- 1/4 teaspoon pepper
- 1 tablespoon minced fresh parsley
- 1 cup each chopped fresh shiitake, baby Portobello and white mushrooms
- 2 garlic cloves, minced
- 1 tablespoon butter

Directions:

1. Preheat the air fryer to 325 °F. Take a small skillet, cook and crumble beef over medium heat until no longer pink, 4-5 minutes. Transfer to a large bowl.

2. Add butter and olive oil in the same skillet and place it over medium-high heat; add garlic and shallot; cook for about 1-2 minutes. Stir in mushrooms and wine; cook until mushrooms are tender. Add to beef mixture along with parsley, salt, and pepper.

3. To make wontons, place about 2 teaspoons filling in the center of each wrapper. Brush egg and water mixture around the outside edges of each wonton; fold opposite corners over filling and press to seal. Place the wontons in a single layer on tray in air fryer basket; spritz with cooking spray.

4. Cook until lightly browned, about 4-5 minutes. Turn; spritz with cooking spray again. Cook until golden brown and crisp, about 4-5 minutes longer. Serve warm or at room temperature.

Per serving: Calories: 42Kcal; Fat: 1g; Carbs: 5g; Protein: 2g; Sugar: 0g; Sodium: 82mg

123. **Beef Turnovers**

Preparation time: 10 minutes

Cooking time: 20 minutes

Servings: 1 dozen

Ingredients:

- 1 pound ground beef

- 1 jar sauerkraut, rinsed, drained and chopped
- 3 tubes refrigerated crescent rolls
- 1 cup shredded Swiss cheese
- 1 medium onion

Directions:

1. In a large skillet, cook the beef and onion over medium heat until the meat isn't pink anymore, 5-7 minutes.

2. Crumble the meat and drain. Add some sauerkraut and cheese. Unroll your crescent roll dough into rectangles and pinch together all of the seams, so there are no holes in your dough.

3. Place about 1/2 cup of cooked beef mixture on top of each rectangle of dough. Bring the corners over to the center and pinch them together to seal up each one before placing them in the air fryer.

4. Cook them for 12-15 minutes until golden brown on each side.

Per serving: Calories: 634Kcal; Fat: 35g; Carbs: 54g; Protein: 27g; Sugar: 14g; Sodium: 1426mg

124. Kofta Kabab

Preparation time: 5 minutes

Cooking time: 30 minutes

Servings: 6

Ingredients:

- 1 pound ground beef
- 1 pound ground lamb
- 1 small onion
- 1/4 cup fresh parsley
- 1 1/2 teaspoon salt
- 1/2 teaspoon nutmeg
- 1/4 teaspoon cinnamon
- 1/4 teaspoon black pepper
- 1/2 teaspoon paprika
- 1 teaspoon allspice
- 2 teaspoons cumin
- 2 garlic cloves

Directions:

1. To make kofta kebabs, mix all ingredients in food processor until smooth.

2. Divide the meat mixture into even sections and shape into kebabs of your liking.

3. Add to the air fryer basket, cook at 380 °F for 1 minutes until golden brown.

Per serving: Calories: 238Kcal; Fat: 15.2g; Carb: 1.8g; Protein: 22g; Sugar: 0.4g; Sodium: 509.6mg

125. Beef and Bean Chimichangas

Preparation time: 15 minutes

Cooking time: 8 minutes

Servings: 10

Ingredients:

- 1 Pound Ground Beef
- 1/2 Cup Refried Beans
- 10 Taco Size Flour Tortillas
- Toppings - Queso Lettuce, Tomato, Sour Cream
- 1/2 Cup Shredded Colby Jack Cheese
- 1 Package Taco Seasoning

Directions:

1. Brown ground beef in a skillet on medium-high heat. Add taco seasoning as instructed, then add refried beans and mix with the meat.

2. Fill each tortilla with the mixture and top with shredded cheese. Fold each tortilla in half, so that all of its contents are contained inside.

3. Spray one side of each chimichanga (or taco) with non-stick cooking spray or olive oil spray and place them seam side down into your air fryer basket or cooking bowl.

4. Cook at 360°F for 8 minutes, or until they are golden brown on top.

5. Check on them every 5 minutes to make sure they are not burning on the bottom.

Per serving: Calories: 580Kcal; Fat: 22g; Carb: 66g; Protein: 29g; Sugar: 4g; Sodium: 986mg

126. Turkey Tenderloin

Preparation time: 5 minutes

Cooking time: 25 minutes

Servings: 4

Ingredients:

- 1.5-pound turkey tenderloins
- 1 tablespoon Italian seasoning
- salt and pepper

Directions:

1. Preheat your air fryer to 350°F.

2. Sprinkle the Italian seasoning, salt, and pepper on the turkey; place it in the air fryer and cook for 25 minutes, flipping once.

3. The internal temperature of the turkey should be 165°F when it is done.

Per serving: Calories: 168Kcal; Fat: 2g; Carbs: 0g; Protein: 34g; Sugar: 0g; Sodium: 162mg

127. Chicken Fajita

Preparation time: 10 minutes

Cooking time: 10 minutes

Servings: 4

Ingredients:

- 1/2 pound boneless and skinless chicken breasts
- 1 medium red onion
- 1 tablespoon chili powder
- 1 teaspoon cumin
- Salt and pepper to taste
- 2 teaspoons lime juice
- 1 tablespoon Corn Oil
- 1 large red or yellow bell pepper

Directions:

1. Preheat your air fryer to 370°F. Put the chicken strips, bell pepper, onions, and cumin in a bowl with Mazola Corn Oil, chili powder, lime juice, salt, and pepper.

2. Mix well. Place the fajitas in the air fryer basket and cook for 10-13 minutes.

3. Remove fajitas from the air fryer when they reach 165°F at their thickest point. Warm tortillas if needed, and enjoy!

Per serving: Calories: 155Kcal; Fat: 6g; Carbs: 7g; Protein: 19g; Sugar: 1g; Sodium: 176mg

128. Turkey Bacon

Preparation time: 6 minutes

Cooking time: 6 minutes

Servings: 4

Ingredients:

- 8 Slices of turkey bacon

Directions:

1. To cook turkey bacon in an air fryer, preheat the appliance to 400°F. Place the bacon in the machine and cook for 5 to 6 minutes.

2. Cook uncured bacon that's a little wider for about 8 to 9 minutes. Flip the bacon halfway through cooking.

Per serving: Calories: 60Kcal; Fat: 4g; Carbs: 1g; Protein: 5g; Sugar: 1g; Sodium: 327mg

129. Chicken Breast

Preparation time: 2 minutes

Cooking time: 10 minutes

Servings: 4

Ingredients:

- 4 boneless chicken breasts
- 1/4 teaspoon garlic powder
- Salt and Pepper
- 2 tablespoons butter

Directions:

1. Preheat your air fryer to 380°F. Place boneless chicken breasts on a cutting board and drizzle with melted butter. Mix in garlic powder, salt, and pepper; then coat both sides of each breast with the mixture.

2. Place the chicken into the air fryer basket and cook for 10-15 minutes, flipping halfway through cooking. The chicken should read 165°F at its thickest part when done.

3. Let rest for 5 minutes before enjoying it.

Per serving: Calories: 250Kcal; Fat: 10g; Carbs: 0g;
Protein: 37g; Sugar: 0g; Sodium: 399mg

CHAPTER 6: Desserts

130. Air-Fryer Brownies

Preparation time: 5 minutes

Cooking time: 15 minutes

Servings: 4

Ingredients:

- ½ cup all-purpose flour
- ¾ cup sugar
- 2 large eggs
- ½ teaspoon vanilla extract
- ¼ teaspoon baking powder
- ¼ teaspoon salt
- 1 Tablespoon vegetable oil
- ¼ cup unsalted butter melted
- 6 Tablespoon unsweetened cocoa powder

Directions:

1. First, preheat the Air Fryer by setting the temperature to 330°F and allowing it to run for about 5 minutes.

2. While this is happening, prepare a brownie batter: Add all-purpose flour, cocoa powder, sugar, butter, eggs, vegetable oil, vanilla extract, and salt into a large bowl and stir until thoroughly combined.

3. Pour over the prepared baking pan and smooth out the top with a spatula.

4. Bake for 15 minutes or until you insert a toothpick into the center and it comes out mostly clean.

5. Remove the brownie from the pan and allow it to cool before removing it from the pan and cutting into squares.

Per serving: Calories: 385Kcal; Fat: 18g; Carbs: 54g; Protein: 6g; Sugar: 38g; Sodium: 181mg

131. Chocolate Chip Oatmeal Cookie

Preparation time: 20 minutes

Cooking time: 10 minutes

Servings: 6

Ingredients:

- 1 cup butter, softened
- 3/4 cup packed brown sugar
- 1 teaspoon vanilla extract
- 1-1/2 cups all-purpose flour
- 1 teaspoon baking soda
- 2 cups semisweet chocolate chips
- 1 cup chopped nuts
- 1 teaspoon salt
- 1 package instant vanilla pudding mix
- 3 cups quick-cooking oats
- 2 large eggs
- 3/4 cup sugar

Directions:

1. Preheat air fryer to 325°F. Take a large bowl, and mix cream butter and sugars until light, well combined, and fluffy, about 5 minutes.

2. Beat in eggs and vanilla. In another bowl, stir oats and flour; gradually beat into a creamed mixture.

3. Stir in chocolate chips and nuts; drop dough by tablespoonsful onto baking sheets.

4. Cook until lightly browned 8-10 minutes or until cooked through.

5. Remove from oven to wire racks to cool; repeat with remaining batter if necessary.

Per serving: Calories: 102Kcal; Fat: 5g; Carbs: 13g; Protein: 2g; Sugar: 8g; Sodium: 82mg

132. Midnight Nutella Banana Sandwich

Preparation time: 5 minutes

Cooking time: 8 minutes

Servings: 2

Ingredients:

- 4 Slices of bread
- ¼ Cup chocolate hazelnut spread
- 1 banana

Directions:

1. First, preheat the air fryer to 370°F. Spread softened butter on half of one bread slice, then place the other bread slice, buttered side down on top.

2. Spread chocolate hazelnut spread on the other half of bread slice, and then place a banana half on each piece of bread.

3. Cut each half into three pieces lengthwise and place them on two slices of bread with remaining bread slices making two sandwiches.

4. Cut in half(triangle or rectangle)to fit in air fryer at once. Transfer sandwiches to a hot ring and fry for 5 minutes until browned.

5. Flip over sandwiches and fry for another 2 to 3 minutes or until desired crispiness is reached. Pour yourself a glass of milk or nightcap while waiting for sandwiches to cool slightly. Enjoy!!

Per serving: Calories: 388Kcal; Fat: 13g; Carbs: 61g; Protein: 7g; Sugar: 30g; Sodium: 261mg

133. Baked Molten Lava Cake

Preparation time: 5 minutes

Cooking time: 10 minutes

Servings: 4

Ingredients:

- 1.5 Tablespoon Self-Rising Flour
- 3.5 Tablespoon Baker's Sugar
- 3.5 OZ Unsalted Butter
- 3.5 OZ Dark Chocolate

- 2 Eggs

Directions:

1. Grease and flour four standard oven-saf ramekins. Melt chocolate and butter in a bowl tha is microwave safe for about 3 minutes, stir continuously so that chocolate and butter are we combined.

2. Whisk/beat the eggs and sugar until pale an frothy. Pour melted chocolate mixture into eg mixture. Stir in flour, using a spatula to combin everything evenly.

3. Pour the cake mixture into ramekins, and bak in a preheated air fryer at 375°F for 10 minute. Remove from the air fryer, let cool for 2 minute inside each ramekin (or just 1 minute if usin silicone ones), then turn upside down onto servin plate or platter (tapping the bottom of eac ramekin with a butter knife to loosen edges necessary).

4. Cake should release from ramekin with littl effort, and the center should appear dark/gooe once served warm a la mode or drizzled wit raspberry sauce

Per serving: Calories: 526Kcal; Fat: 40g; Carb: 36g; Protein: 6g; Sugar: 26g; Sodium: 31mg

134. Shortbread

Preparation time: 10 minutes

Cooking time: 8 minutes

Servings: 6

Ingredients:

- 250 g Self Raising Flour
- 175 g Butter
- 75 g Sugar

Directions:

1. First, make a soft shortbread dough by rubbin butter into flour and sugar until it resemble breadcrumbs. If you haven't done so already, us a knife to chop the butter into tiny bits. Then ru

the fat into the flour and sugar using your hands. Rub until it resembles breadcrumbs.

2. Then combine them together with your fingers until they form a soft dough.

3. Flour a clean kitchen worktop and flour a rolling pin too; then roll out your shortbread dough to about 0.5cm thick. Then cut out shapes depending on their desired size.

4. Then add a layer of foil into the air fryer basket and then place the shortbread over it.

5. Finally, air fry for almost 8 minutes at 180°C/360°F, then allow it to cool completely before storing in an airtight container.

Per serving: Calories: 408Kcal; Fat: 24g; Carbs: 43g; Protein: 5g; Sugar: 13g; Sodium: 209mg

135. Apple Pie

Preparation time: minutes

Cooking time: minutes

Servings:

Ingredients:

- 1 tablespoon raw sugar
- 1 tablespoon butter
- 2 tablespoon sugar
- 2 teaspoons lemon juice
- Baking spray
- 1 Pillsbury Refrigerator pie crust
- 1 large apple, chopped
- 1 tablespoon ground cinnamon
- ½ teaspoon vanilla extract
- 1 beaten egg

Directions:

1. To make your pie crust, you'll need to defrost the frozen dessert before cooking it. To do this, preheat your Air Fryer while you prepare the pie.

2. Place the smaller baking tin upside down on a flat surface and put another baking pan inside to catch any drips.

3. Then, take one of the pie crusts out of its package and place it into the smaller baking tin so

that it fits snugly in there. Press firmly on top of the pie and smooth out any folds with your fingers or a rolling pin.

4. Once you've done this, set the smaller pie aside while working on the other. Spray a small bowl with cooking spray, add chopped apples and lemon juice along with cinnamon powder, sugar, and vanilla extract; mix everything well and pour into a larger pie pan sprayed with cooking spray.

5. Place second pie crust over the top of apples in the pan and pinch edges together to seal. Make slits on top of dough near the edge for vents so that steam doesn't escape during the cooking process.

Per serving: Calories: 57Kcal; Fat: 2g; Carbs: 6g; Protein: 3g; Sugar: 1g; Sodium: 45mg

136. Thai Fried Bananas

Preparation time: 20 minutes

Cooking time: 40 minutes

Servings: 4

Ingredients:

- 4 Ripe Bananas
- 2 tablespoons Rice flour
- 2 tablespoons Desiccated Coconut
- 1/2 teaspoon Baking powder
- Oil , to drizzle
- Sesame seeds
- 1/4 cup Rice flour
- 1/2 teaspoon Cardamom Powder
- 1 pinch Salt
- 2 tablespoons Corn flour
- 2 tablespoons All-Purpose Flour

Directions:

1. To make fried bananas, gather the ingredients together and keep them handy. We'll begin by making the batter for the fried bananas.

2. Add all-purpose flour, rice flour, corn flour, baking powder, salt, and coconut into a large bowl, and stir to combine well. Add a little amount

of water at a time until you get a thick and almost smooth batter.

3. Coat the banana slices in batter and roll them in rice flour and sesame seeds.

4. Then place them in a greased foil or butter paper for air frying at 200°C for almost 10 – 15 minutes until golden browned. Serve with ice cream for dessert.

Per serving: Calories: 191Kcal; Fat: 5.7g; Carbs: 37g; Protein: 1.59g; Sugar: 20g; Sodium: 12.1mg

137. Apple Crisp

Preparation time: 5 minutes

Cooking time: 25 minutes

Servings: 2

Ingredients:

- 2 chopped apples
- 1 teaspoon of cinnamon
- 1 Teaspoon of lemon juice
- 2 tablespoons of brown sugar

For Topping

- 2 ½ tablespoons of flour
- 1 pinch of salt
- 2 tablespoons of cold butter
- 3 tablespoons of old-fashioned oats
- 2 tablespoons of brown sugar

Directions:

1. First, preheat the air fryer to 350°F. Butter a 5-inch oval baking dish. Peel the apples and chop them into small pieces.

2. Combine the apples with lemon juice, sugar, and cinnamon in a bowl. Pour into the dish and cover it with aluminum foil.

3. Bake for 15 minutes at 350°F, then uncover and continue cooking for 5 more minutes until golden brown on top.

4. To make topping: combine flour, sugar, salt, oats, and cold butter in an electric mixer fitted

with the paddle attachment and mix on low speed until mixture crumbles into small pieces.

5. Scatter evenly over apples; place crisp back in air fryer uncovered for another 5 minutes to melt butter; enjoy warm with some melted caramel sauce on top or whipped cream!

Per serving: Calories: 355Kcal; Fat: 13g; Carbs: 61.5g; Protein: 3.3g; Sugar: 37.5g; Sodium: mg

138. Cinnamon Sugar Dessert Fries

Preparation time: 5 minutes

Cooking time: 15 minutes

Servings: 4

Ingredients:

- 2 sweet potatoes
- 1 tablespoon butter
- 1/2 teaspoon cinnamon
- 2 tablespoons sugar

Directions:

1. Preheat your air fryer to 380°F. Peel and cut the sweet potatoes into thin fries.

2. Coat the fries with 1 tablespoon of butter, then cook them in the preheated air fryer for 15-18 minutes. They should not fill your air fryer more than 1/2 full and should overlap one another so they do not burn on the outside before they are cooked through on the inside.

3. When they are done cooking, remove them and place them into a bowl with 1 teaspoon of butter and 1 teaspoon of brown sugar, then mix well. They are ready to eat immediately!

Per serving: Calories: 110Kcal; Fat: 4g; Carbs: 18g; Protein: 1g; Sugar: 10g; Sodium: 51mg

139. Air-Fryer Oreo

Preparation time: 2 minutes

Cooking time: 8 minutes

Servings: 8

Ingredients:

- 1 can Crescents Dough

- 8 Oreo cookies
- 1-2 tablespoons Powdered Sugar

Directions:

1. To make your own Oreo cookies, you will need to create a cookie dough. To do this, simply open up a package of Oreos and cover each piece with the dough until it is completely covered.

2. Place these covered cookies onto an air fryer rack and cook them at 350°F for 4 minutes on the lowest setting.

3. Once they have been flipped once, remove them from the rack and continue to cook them until you see they are golden brown on both sides.

4. Once they are done, sprinkle them with powdered sugar before serving.

Per serving: Calories: 159Kcal; Fat: 8g; Carbs: 21g; Protein: 2g; Sugar: 9g; Sodium: 277mg

140. Banana Bread

Preparation time: 15 minutes

Cooking time: 45 minutes

Servings: 8

Ingredients:

- 3/4 cup white-whole wheat flour
- 1/2 teaspoon salt
- 2 medium ripe bananas
- 1/2 cup granulated sugar
- 2 tablespoons vegetable oil
- 2 tablespoons toasted walnuts
- 1 teaspoon cinnamon
- 1/4 teaspoon Baking soda
- 2 large eggs
- 1/3 cup plain yogurt
- 1 teaspoon Vanilla extract
- Cooking spray

Directions:

1. Take a 6-inch round cake pan and coat it with cooking spray. Mix flour, cinnamon, salt, and baking soda together in a medium bowl.

2. Whisk together mashed bananas, eggs, sugar, and yogurt in another medium bowl. Gently pour wet ingredients into the flour mixture and mix them until well combined.

3. Pour the batter into the coated pan and sprinkle with walnuts before putting it in the air fryer.

4. Heat at 310°F for 30 to 35 minutes or until browned and a wooden pick inserted in the middle comes out clean; turn halfway through cook time.

5. Transfer bread to a wire rack to cool before turning out of pan and slicing into pieces.

Per serving: Calories: 180Kcal; Fat: 6g; Carbs: 29g; Protein: 4g; Sugar: 13g; Sodium: 184mg

141. Chocolate Cake

Preparation time: 5 minutes

Cooking time: 10 minutes

Servings: 6

Ingredients:

- 1 & 1/2 Cups Almond Flour
- 1/3 Cup Unsweetened Cocoa Powder
- 2 Large Eggs
- 1 Teaspoon Baking Powder
- 1/2 Cup Powdered Swerve
- 1/3 Cup Unsweetened Almond Milk
- 1 Teaspoon Vanilla Extract
- 1/4 Teaspoon Salt

Directions:

1. To make your own air fryer cakes, combine all ingredients in a large mixing bowl and mix until well combined.

2. Spray or butter the pan(s) of your choice, then scoop batter into each pan.

3. Set the heat to 350°F and set your timer for 10 minutes.

4. Cake(s) should be done when a toothpick enters into the center comes out clean.

Per serving: Calories: 207Kcal; Fat: 17.2g; Carbs: 3.4g; Protein: 8.1g; Sugar: 7g; Sodium: mg

142. Cheese Cake

Preparation time: 15 minutes

Cooking time: 35 minutes

Servings: 12

Ingredients:

- 750 g Soft Cheese
- 3 Large Eggs
- 1 Tablespoon Vanilla Essence
- 90 g Biscuits
- 400 g Caster Sugar
- 50 ml Greek Yoghurt
- 75 g Melted Butter

Directions:

1. To make this cheesecake, you'll need to start by assembling your ingredients. First, put the butter into an air fryer baking pan and set it to 120°C/250°F. Next, add in your biscuits and break them down a bit so they will blend into crumbs easily.

2. Then add some melted butter over the top of the biscuits and press down on the bottom of the spring form pan to get everything to stick together.

3. Now let's move on to adding our other ingredients!

4. Add the softened cheese and vanilla essence and stir again.

5. Pat down the cheesecake mixture over the top of a spring form pan, then set aside in the fridge until ready to serve.

Per serving: Calories: 447Kcal; Fat: 29g; Carbs: 41g; Protein: 6g; Sugar: 37g; Sodium: 302mg

143. Double Glazed Cinnamon Biscuit Bites

Preparation time: 25 minutes

Cooking time: 40 minutes

Servings: 8

Ingredients:

- 2/3 cup all-purpose flour
- 2 tablespoons granulated sugar
- 1/4 teaspoon ground cinnamon
- 4 tablespoons cold salted butter
- Cooking spray
- 3 tablespoons water
- 2/3 cup whole-wheat flour
- 1 teaspoon baking powder
- 1/4 teaspoon kosher salt
- 1/3 cup whole milk
- 2 cups powdered sugar

Directions:

1. Sift together flour, sugar, baking powder, cinnamon, and salt in a medium bowl.

2. Cut butter into mixture using 2 knives or pastry cutter until butter is well combined with flour and the mixture resembles coarse cornmeal.

3. Add milk and mix together until dough turns into a ball. Place dough on floured surface; knead until smooth and cohesive—about 30 seconds.

4. Cut into 16 equal pieces. Roll each piece of dough with lighter hand and turn into balls.

5. Coat air fryer basket well with cooking spray; place 8 balls in basket leaving room between each; spray donut balls with cooking spray. Cook at 350°F until browned and puffed—about 10-1 minutes.

6. Gently remove donut balls from basket; place on wire rack over foil to cool 5 minutes before glazing again with remaining glaze

Per serving: Calories: 325Kcal; Fat: 7g; Carbs: 60g Protein: 8g; Sugar: 18g; Sodium: 67mg

144. Deep Fried Snickers

Preparation time: 10 minutes

Cooking time: 6 minutes

Servings: 10

Ingredients:

- 10 Fun Size Snickers Bars
- 8 oz Crescent Rolls Tube

• 1 Tablespoon Butter, melted

Directions:

1. To make chocolate-dipped snickers, remove crescent rolls from the tube, unroll dough, and place on baking sheet.

2. Cut out 10 squares; wrap each one with a piece of dough. Pinch seams and cuts well to seal completely.

3. Brush dough with melted butter and place on baking sheet.

4. Air Fry at 370°F for 6 minutes or until golden brown. Top with powdered sugar, whipped cream, and drizzle on chocolate sauce.

Per serving: Calories: 67Kcal; Fat: 4g; Carbs: 8g; Protein: 1g; Sugar: 3g; Sodium: 119mg

145. Air-Fryer Scones

Preparation time: 10 minutes

Cooking time: 7 minutes

Servings: 6

Ingredients:

• 225 g Self Raising Flour
• 28 g Caster Sugar
• Egg Wash
• Squirty Cream
• Strawberry Jam
• 50 g Butter
• 60 ml Whole Milk
• Extra Virgin Olive Oil Spray
• Fresh Strawberries

Directions:

1. Make your scones by combining flour and sugar in a bowl. Add cubed butter and rub it into the flour until it resembles coarse breadcrumbs.

2. Add enough milk to make a soft dough about 60ml.

3. Then roll out your dough on a floured worktop and make sure they are not small. Use cutters to cut your scones into medium-sized portions, then place them in the air fryer basket with a light coating of extra virgin olive oil sprayed on top to prevent them from sticking against each other.

4. Brush each side of the scones with egg wash as well as their tops and sides to give them a nice golden colour before putting them in your air fryer set at 180°C/360°F for 5 minutes followed by another 2 minutes at 160°C/320°F after they have been cooked through completely.

5. Serve with strawberry jam, sliced strawberries, cream, and plenty of orange zest!

Per serving: Calories: 219Kcal; Fat: 8g; Carbs: 32g; Protein: 5g; Sugar: 5g; Sodium: 65mg

146. Chocolate Chip Cookie Bar

Preparation time: 35 minutes

Cooking time: 8 minutes

Servings: 9

Ingredients:

• 1 stick butter softened
• 1 cup chocolate chips
• 1 Teaspoon vanilla
• 1/2 Teaspoon soda
• 1/4 cup white sugar
• 1 and 1/8 cups flour
• Pinch of salt
• Egg

Directions:

1. In a large bowl, beat together softened butter, vanilla, and egg. Stir in sugar and salt. Then stir in flour, baking soda, and chocolate chips.

2. Heat the air fryer to 320°F/160°C. Place the dough in a prepared pan and spread evenly across it. Place the pan into your air fryer.

3. Cook for 7-9 minutes or until the top becomes light brown. Using a kitchen towel, take out the pan when finished cooking and let cool before slicing into bars or cakes of your choice!

Per serving: Calories: 211Kcal; Fat: 14g; Carbs: 19g; Protein: 1g; Sugar: 18g; Sodium: 103mg

147. Peanut Butter banana Dessert Bites

Preparation time: 15 minutes

Cooking time: 6 minutes

Servings: 12

Ingredients:

- 1 large Banana (sliced)
- 1/2 cup Peanut Butter
- 1 Oil Mister
- 12 Won Ton Wrappers
- 1-2 tsp Vegetable Oil
- Semi-Sweet Chocolate Chips
- M&M's
- Raisins
- Ground Cinnamon
- Lemon juice

Directions:

1. Slice a banana and put it in a bowl of water along with a splash of lemon juice to keep it from browning. Place one slice of banana in the middle of a won ton wrapper, then add peanut butter on top.

2. Brush water along the edges of the wrapper and bring together opposite corners to form a tube.

3. Squeeze out any excess water inside the wrapper and fold up the remaining opposite sides so that they meet in the middle.

4. Place it into an air fryer basket, spritz it with oil, and then cook for 6 minutes at 380°F.

5. Serve with vanilla ice cream and sprinkle with cinnamon and sugar if desired.

Per serving: Calories: 309Kcal; Fat: 11g; Carbs: 46g; Protein: 10g; Sugar: 13g; Sodium: 334mg

148. Funnel Cake

Preparation time: 10 minutes

Cooking time: 5 minutes

Servings: 4

Ingredients:

- 1 Cup White Self-Rising Flour
- 1 Teaspoon Vanilla Extract
- Cooking Spray
- 1 Cup Plain Greek yogurt
- 1/2 Teaspoon Ground Cinnamon
- 1 1/2 Tablespoon Powdered Sugar

Directions:

1. First, combine the yogurt, vanilla, cinnamon, and flour in a bowl. Mix until well combined.

2. Then knead the dough for 2 minutes on a floured surface. If it's sticky, add flour a small amount at a time until it's easy to knead.

3. Next, prepare a work surface by putting down some parchment paper and dusting it with flour. Put the dough on the paper and cut it into 4 equal sections. Working with one of those sections, roll it out into a rope that is about 8-10 inches long. Repeat this process with the other 3 sections.

4. Now pile up your ropes of dough and shape them loosely into a funnel cake shape without letting them drop off the end or touch each other or their edges.

Per serving: Calories: 160Kcal; Fat: 1g; Carbs: 29g; Protein: 9g; Sugar: 5g; Sodium: 393mg

149. Chocolate Hazelnut Turnovers

Preparation time: 10 minutes

Cooking time: 10 minutes

Servings: 12

Ingredients:

- 1 frozen puff pastry sheet
- 3 tablespoons chopped hazelnuts
- Powdered sugar
- ⅓ cup chocolate-hazelnut spread
- 1 egg

Directions:

1. To make the turnovers, preheat the air fryer to 400°F. Line a baking sheet with parchment paper and lightly flour it. Make sure you have an extra-large bowl of ice water nearby.

2. Place one sheet of puff pastry on a floured surface, then roll it out until it is 9 x 12 inches in size. With a sharp knife cut each piece into 3 x 3-inch squares. In one of the centers of each square, place about 1 teaspoon chocolate hazelnut spread and sprinkle with hazelnuts.

3. Fold each triangle in half diagonally so that it forms a triangle that looks like a diamond. Brush the edges of each triangle with egg mixture and press together to seal them in place.

4. Arrange these triangles on their baking sheet and repeat until all pieces are done.

Per serving: Calories: 144Kcal; Fat: 9g; Carbs: 14g; Protein: 3g; Sugar: 6g; Sodium: 79mg

30 Days Meal Plan

Days	Breakfast	Lunch	Dinner
Day 1	Hard-Boiled Eggs + a cup of milk	Chicken Cordon Bleu	Crumbed Fish
Day 2	Breakfast Potatoes	Jamaican Peas and Rice	Pork Chops
Day 3	Air Fried Bacon	Coconut-Crusted Turkey Fingers	Meatloaf
Day 4	Egg in a Hole	Crispy Pork Belly	Green Sauce and Pinto Beans Queso
Day 5	Sausage biscuit	Honey Mustard Salmon	Buttermilk Fried Chicken
Day 6	Prosciutto and Spinach Egg Cups	Turkey Croquettes	Roast Beef
Day 7	Air Fried Bagel	Crispy Chicken Wings	Rack of lamb
Day 8	Homemade Granola	Turkish Chicken Kebab	Green Beans and Potato Fry
Day 9	Crisp Egg Cups	Whole Chicken	Spicy Lamb Sirloin Steak
Day 10			Steak Fajita

	Breakfast pizza sweet Potato Hash + a cup of milk/tea	Beef Kababs with baked veggies	
Day 11	Crispy French Toast	Green Sauce and Pinto Beans Queso	Pecan Crusted Chicken
Day 12	Breakfast Frittata	Rib-Eye Steak with Blue Cheese	Chicken Cordon Bleu
Day 13	Cinnamon Toast	Crumbed Fish	Meatballs
Day 14	Hash Browns + a cup of tea/milk	Coconut-Crusted Turkey Fingers	Gingered Honey Salmon
Day 15	Scotch Eggs + a cup of milk	Turkey Tenderloin	Jamaican Peas and Rice
Day 16	Egg in a Hole	Ultimate Lamb Burgers	Steak Fajita
Day 17	Homemade Granola	Fish Fillet	Turkish Chicken Kebab
Day 18	Scrambled eggs	Beef and Bean Chimichangas	Crispy Chicken Wings
Day 19	Crispy French Toast	Pork Chops	Whole Chicken
Day 20	Crisp Egg Cups	Meatloaf	Breaded Sea Scallops

Day 21	Air Fried Bacon	Spicy Lamb Sirloin Steak	Fish Nuggets
Day 22	Hard-Boiled Eggs + a cup of milk	Red Kidney Beans Pakora	Beef Kababs with baked veggies
Day 23	Cinnamon Toast	Bacon-Wrapped Hot Dogs	Stuffed Meat Loaf Slices
Day 24	Cheesy Baked Eggs	Beef Turnovers	Chicken Breast
Day 25	Sausage biscuit	Ultimate Lamb Burgers	Turkey Bacon
Day 26	Cinnamon Toast	Fish and Chips	Crispy Roasted Lentils
Day 27	Omelet with 1 or 2 slices of bread	Buttermilk Fried Chicken	Steak Fajita
Day 28	Prosciutto and Spinach Egg Cups	Chicken Fajita	Beef Wellington Wontons
Day 29	Scotch Eggs + a cup of milk	Green Beans with Bacons	Crispy Pork Belly
Day 30	Egg rolls	Kofta Kabab	Miso-Glazed Salmon

Air Fryer cook time and Temperature

Let's talk about how long it takes to cook your favorite fried food in an air-fryer? We've made your kitchen tour for you by breaking down the cooking time and temperature for each food type. There are so many delicious dishes you can make in an air-fryer! That's why we've compiled everyone's favorite recipes—from chicken wings to French fries—and decoded how long they'll take in your trusty air fryer.

Meat and Seafood

Bacon	400°F	5-10 minutes
Bone-In Pork Chops	400°F	4-5 minutes per side
Brats	400°F	8-10 minutes
Burgers	350°F	8-10 minutes
Chicken Breast	375°F	22-23 minutes
Chicken Tenders	400°F	14-16 minutes
Chicken Thighs	400°F	25 minutes
Chicken Wings	375°F	10-12 minutes
Cod	370°F	8-10 minutes
Meatballs	400°F	7-10 minutes
Meat Loaf	325°F	35-45 minutes

Pork Chops	375°F	12-15 minutes
Salmon	400°F	5-7 minutes
Sausage Patties	400°F	8-10 minutes
Shrimp	375°F	8 minutes
Steak	400°F	7-14 minutes
Tilapia	400°F	6-8 minutes

Vegetables

Asparagus	375°F	4-6 minutes
Baked Potatoes	400°F	35-45 minutes
Broccoli	400°F	8-10 minutes
Brussels Sprouts	350°F	15-18 minutes
Butternut Squash (cubed)	375°F	20-25 minutes
Carrots	375°F	15-25 minutes
Cauliflower	400°F	10-12 minutes
Green Beans	375°F	16-20 minutes

Peppers	375°F	8-10 minutes
Sweet Potatoes (cubed)	375°F	15-20 minutes
Zucchini	400°F	12 minutes

Fried Foods

Fries	400°F	10-20 minutes
Pickles	400°F	14-20 minutes
Potato Chips	360°F	15-17 minutes

Frozen Foods

Corn Dogs	400°F	8 minutes
Mozzarella Sticks	400°F	6-8 minutes
Tater Tots	400°F	12-15 minutes

Bakes and Breads

Brownies	325°F	40-45 minutes
Cookies	325°F	8-10 minutes
Cupcakes	325°F	11-13 minutes

Garlic Bread	350°F	2-3 minutes

Mains/Snacks

Mini Pizzas	400°F	4-5 minutes
Quesadillas	375°F	5-7 minutes

Conclusion

The recipes in the book are not just for maintaining health problems related to diabetes, but they will keep you healthy without feeling like you have any health issues. The meals are designed to keep your blood sugar levels in check. They are all made in an air-fryer, so you won't have difficulty cooking a single dish. Each recipe is delicious and easy to make. As you follow the recipes, we hope to see your health improve daily!

Recipes Index

Green Tomato Stacks; 22
Halibut; 37
Halibut Pistachio Crusted; 44
Hard-Boiled Eggs; 8
Hash Browns; 8
Herb and Lemon Cauliflower; 17
Homemade Granola; 11
Honey Glazed Salmon; 37
Honey Mustard Salmon; 39
Kidney Bean Popcorn; 25
Kofta Kabab; 58
Lemon Pepper Green Beans; 34
Lobster Tails; 43
Midnight Nutella Banana Sandwich; 62
Miso Glazed Chilean Sea Bass; 42
Miso-Glazed Salmon; 39
Okra with Smoked Paprika; 18
Peanut Butter banana Dessert Bites; 68
Pepper Poppers; 22
Perfect Cinnamon Toast; 12
Pork Chops; 49; 51
Portobello Melts; 21
Potato Chips; 16
Potatoes with Green Beans; 31
Prosciutto and Spinach Egg Cups; 10
Rack of Lamb; 54
Radishes; 19
Red Kidney Beans Pakora; 25; 72
Rib-Eye Steak with Blue Cheese; 56
Roast Beef; 53

Roasted Garlic Green Beans; 33
Roasted Green Beans; 16
Salmon Patties; 40
Salmon with Maple Soy Glaze; 42
Sausage biscuit; 9
Scallops with Garlic Herb Butter; 41
Scrambled Eggs; 13
Shortbread; 62
Shrimp (Honey Lime); 37
Shrimp Fajita; 44
Shrimp Tacos; 38
Sichuan-Style Green Beans; 33
Soft-Boiled Scotch Eggs; 12
Spicy Asian Green Beans; 34
Spicy Green Beans; 20; 28
Steak Fajitas; 49
Stuffed Meat Loaf Slices; 56
Sweet Potato; 17
Sweet Potato Hash; 14
Sweet Potato Nachos; 20
Thai Fried Bananas; 63
Tuna Cakes; 38
Tuna Melt; 40
Turkey Bacon; 59
Turkey Croquettes; 48
Turkey Tenderloin; 58
Turkish Chicken Kebab; 52
Ultimate Lamb Burgers; 54
Whole Chicken; 53

Made in the USA
Las Vegas, NV
11 October 2023

78872356R00044